Praise for
Meta-Brain

"Alexandrea has done what the fields of neuroscience and psychology have been struggling to do for years: Create a self-guided model for self-healing. This book is the next step in the evolution of neuropsychology and global healing."

—Dr. Chris Lee,
Neuroscience Researcher and Educator, Biometric Health Analyst, CEO of Elemental Shift Consulting

"Alexandrea 'jumps right in' to a new realm of self-help in this book. Adaptive Therapy is the new frontier for mental health, and Alexandrea is at the forefront!"

—Ed Krow,
Talent Transformation Expert

"*Meta-Brain* is way more than a book. It is a journey to the mysterious wonderland hidden between 'stimulus' and 'response.' In this current age of need, greed, and speed, human life is ceaselessly stretched between actions and reactions. Ms. Day coaches the reader to breathe easy and pause. Honest, articulate, and witty, she demonstrates her insights with anecdotes from her career-long practice in Adaptive Therapy. Life can be reinvented [at] any time on a landscape of new beliefs and possibilities. I turned the last page, empowered and enlightened, and realized that this book would not rest idly on my desk. It will now travel to my friends and family and change their lives, too. Well, I'll take it back. They will transform their own lives from mere survival to complete engagement. That is living life powerfully—rich with freedom, intent, and excellence."

—Dr. Pabitra K. (PK) Chakrabarti,
JD, Ph.D., Patent Counsel and Technology Evangelist

"A delightful, must-read book taking you on a healing journey of self-discovery based on the interconnectedness between neuroscience and human emotions. Being a neuroscientist myself, I was very fortunate to work closely with the author and her team during the validation of Adaptive Theory, where we used cutting-edge scientific methods to uncover the neural basis of the unconscious, allowing us to open a novel path to emotional awareness and well-being."

—Yanina Tsenkina, Ph.D.,
CEO (CYC Biomedical Consulting)

"Adaptive Therapy's ability to reprogram the body's stress response brings a new wave of understanding to the field of CBT. Innovative therapy drives will increase well-being and reduce our risk of developing a stress-induced disease. Having individual control of one's own stress response system is an innovation greatly needed as our world increasingly bears down on us."

—Lorelei Walker,
Ph.D. MPH, Director of Public Health Training,
Social Safety Initiative

"I was introduced to Adaptive Therapy in 1996, felt an immediate shift in my soul, and have used it ever since. I absolutely credit it for changing me and enabling me to create a different life than the one I was living."

—Gail Wailes,
Certified Adaptive Therapist

"Adaptive Therapy stands to enliven and empower the field of psychology like nothing that's come before it. The potential to improve the well-being and overall life satisfaction of individuals the world over can hardly be overstated if this technique continues to be practiced, taught, and well researched. Adaptive Therapy offers a vast spectrum of opportunities not only for the client but also for the keen psychology researcher, the innovative technologist, or the insightful entrepreneur. This client-empowering self-healing approach to wellness could prove to be a major pivot point in the future of healthcare and human potential."

—Tom Hunden,
MS, Director IAffirm

"Alex's work has evolved over many years, and she has helped so many people. I will always be grateful to her for freeing me from Chronic Fatigue and many other issues. May her work continue to help many people around the world."

—Pam Hawes,
Client

Meta-Brain

Reprogramming the Unconscious for Self-Directed Living

Alexandrea Day

MADE FOR
SUCCESS

Made for Success Publishing
P.O. Box 1775 Issaquah, WA 98027
www.MadeForSuccessPublishing.com

This book is not intended to be a substitute for medical or mental health advice from a licensed professional. The reader should consult with their doctor or therapist in any matters relating to his/her health.

Distributed by Made for Success Publishing

First Printing

Library of Congress Cataloging-in-Publication data
Day, Alexandrea
      Meta-Brain: Reprogramming the Unconscious for Self-Directed Living
      p. cm.

    LCCN: 2022905610
    ISBN: 978-1-64146-715-5 (*Paperback*)
    ISBN: 978-1-64146-716-2 (*eBook*)
    ISBN: 978-1-64146-717-9 (*Audiobook*)

Printed in the United States of America

For further information contact Made for Success Publishing
+14256570300 or email service@madeforsuccess.net

Contents

FOREWORD

As an inventor myself in the area of photographic presentation, including 3D innovation and the first tool to colorize digital film production (eliminating chemicals), I believe this book is likely to be the beginning of a new part of history. Alexandrea brings to the present the common-place tools and methods of the future that allow people to reprogram their minds to achieve individual and collective greatness.

There are moments in life when someone profoundly expands our views or brings life-changing enlightenment. The first time Alexandrea and I met, I experienced a transformative paradigm shift. She is truly amazing and shares her insights and innovations at the intersection of the human mind and cutting-edge technology in a truly revolutionizing manner. As I listened to her vision, I was in awe of her insights, and as two people that have shared Seattle most of our lives, we discovered amazing synergies.

In her book, *Meta-Brain*, Alexandrea highlights the misalignment of advancements and the human ability to keep pace. By reprogramming the unconscious for self-directed living, Alex teaches us the path to adapting effectively to our world. Her approach with Adaptive Therapy addresses the cause of ills and shortsightedness and will contribute greatly to the healing that our world needs.

My favorite aspect of *Meta-Brain* is the guidance it offers for humans to gracefully move within their environment, truly offering adaptive tools to not only keep up but to lead toward a better future.

Alexandrea has spent decades working with thousands of clients, teaching hundreds the Adaptive Therapy process through her Washington State Licensed Vocational School, and traveled globally to teach these techniques to individuals, healthcare professionals, and licensed therapists, and it shows. Her passion is to help counterbalance the downside of stress and exhaustion that technology has brought to the human experience, and her findings are truly remarkable.

It's incredibly refreshing to see a fellow visionary solve for the cause of disease instead of just offering coping skills as so many do.

I'm honored to write this Foreword because this book opens the door to a new era as Alexandrea takes us on a new journey to help us all live from within.

David Austreng,
Owner of Image Technology Laboratories

CHAPTER 1

The Purpose

This book was created to introduce Adaptive Therapy to those who want to access their inner knowing to heal themselves, as well as therapists who seek a tool to precisely identify the client's perceptions and core issues that cause cognitive dissonance. Adaptive Therapy effectively addresses and helps in the resolution of relationship problems by revealing conflicted programming from past experiences that, when triggered, enter into current situations. It is also effective for improving performance in any area of life, whether in sports, work, or learning. When one considers the scope of this tool, the urgency to make it available to all is apparent. In particular, there is a desperate need for emotional healing today due to the widespread effects of the COVID-19 pandemic, including the social and economic restrictions most people have endured.

Adaptive Therapy dives deep into the psyche and the "why" behind individuals' actions and reactions. It emphasizes accessing unconscious personal truths and identifying triggers from past traumas. Then, a person can reprogram their brain to view things in a positive light rather than a negative one, tackling core beliefs, dysfunctional assumptions, and negative automatic thoughts.

The goal of this book, then, is to help the reader grasp the depth and impact of Adaptive Therapy in the lives of those who practice it. Adaptive Therapy is a daily practice of self-assessment that facilitates healing in all areas of life and within all aspects of self. Adaptive Therapy is aimed at living your own purpose in way best suited to who you really are, including your talents, experiences, and inherited genes. It involves being present, paying attention, identifying beliefs that may be faulty, and working with a therapist to assist with self-discovery and metamorphosis.

Scope of Adaptive Therapy

The scope of this book encompasses the emotional aspect of Adaptive Therapy, with a focus on healing the emotional cause affecting the body and the mind. Healing for this purpose also means supporting the body throughout the process. There are many supportive measures that anyone dedicated to health and well-being can use to enhance Adaptive Therapy techniques.

Accessing unconscious personal truth through Adaptive Therapy to learn the "why" of your thoughts and actions, is powerful. Suppose you just got married and, as soon as the ceremony ends, you find yourself in a state of complete rage. With Adaptive Therapy, in about five minutes you can find out why you felt that way, and better yet, have the tools to change it. It is likely that your current feelings of rage have nothing to do with your current mate or the wedding but are instead related to a past experience that has similar elements. The current experience is only triggering a past one. Using Adaptive Therapy techniques, you can quickly determine what past event or trauma is being triggered by the current situation. Then you can clear the old event of its emotional charge, reverse the belief system that is producing the feeling of rage, and if need be, sever the projection onto the current person/experience from the past person/experience.

What Is the Cognitive Model behind Adaptive Therapy?

Adaptive Therapy fits under the Cognitive-Behavioral Therapy (CBT) umbrella as a psychological therapy. CBT has been reported as the most effective method available to clients to discover and alter negative behavior, turning into behavior that leads to well-being (Graske, 2010). It is based on the cognitive model of mental illness, initially developed by Beck (1964). The CBT model suggests that people's emotions and behaviors are influenced by their perceptions of events and not by the actual events themselves. This means that people can experience the same event and yet have completely different perceptions based upon past experience, their knowledge base, and whether or not they have experienced the same event before (Beck, 1964).

Fundamental to the cognitive model is the way in which cognition (the way people think about things and the content of these thoughts) is conceptualized. Beck outlined three levels of cognition (Beck 1976):

- Core beliefs
- Dysfunctional assumptions
- Negative automatic thoughts

Core beliefs are perceptions about self, others, and the world. Core beliefs make up a person's identity, are generally learned early in life, and are influenced by childhood experiences and traumas throughout life.

According to CBT, dysfunctional assumptions are rigid and conditional "rules for living" that people adopt. These may be unrealistic and, therefore, maladaptive. For example, one may live by the rule that "It's better not to try than to risk failing." Using the Adaptive Therapy perspective, a therapist would ask why a client has chosen to believe this, in order to discover the core belief underlying it. In fact, Adaptive Therapy seeks to identify the original event and the original feeling assigned to it, as originally perceived.

So, a therapist would ask, "Why do you feel_____(the feeling) when you experience_____(the event)?" to drill down into the person's unconscious association with the event. Once the therapist has identified the dysfunctional assumptions, Adaptive Therapy creates a de-programming affirmation to uproot the old perception, and then helps the client to re-program their thoughts with what they would like to believe instead. The client applies these new beliefs while practicing mindfulness over a period of a couple of weeks to make a permanent change in thoughts and behavior. Thousands of people have benefited from Adaptive Therapy, as reported anecdotally. New research is underway to validate these anecdotal stories of success.

In CBT, negative automatic thoughts (NATs) are thoughts that individuals involuntarily experience in certain situations. In Adaptive Therapy, these situations are called "triggers" because they bubble up into consciousness feelings associated with a past experience, triggered by a current similar event. In fact, this feeling link (emotion) is the pathway to the person's core belief. CBT helps to connect the dots between the current event triggering the emotion, and the past experience tagged with the same emotion. Identifying this connection will lead the way to identifying the core belief.

In CBT, a formulation process is used to understand the causes, precipitants, and maintaining influences of a person's problems (Eels, 1997). The formulation process is intended to aid the therapist and the client in making sense of the individual's experience, which can lead to mutual understanding of the individual's difficulties. Formulations can be developed using different formats, exemplified by different ways of formulating experiences. Depression is one example of this. Beck et al. (1979) created a longitudinal formulation of depression. Within this formulation, early experiences contribute to the development of core beliefs, which lead to the development of dysfunctional assumptions that are later activated following an event, which produces depression.

Formulations can also be cross-sectional. For example, the "hot-cross bun model" (Greenberger & Padesky, 1995) emphasizes how an individual's thoughts, feelings, behavior, and physical symptoms interact. Adaptive Therapy has also found a link between physical symptoms and emotional states. Many clients experience quick dissipation of physical symptoms upon the reversal of a core belief, which removes their emotional attachment to it. Research is in the early phases in this field, but anecdotal experience demonstrates a direct correlation between how we feel emotionally and how we feel physically, with one affecting the other.

The formulation process in Adaptive Therapy holds that humans are programmed with thousands of perceptions that produce angst if they are violated. An example of violating a core belief would be if you are called on to speak spontaneously in front of a group, and this triggers a core belief like, "I need to be quiet." This trigger results in intense feelings such as being terrified and feeling like vomiting; your hands start sweating and you are overwhelmed by a feeling of light-headedness. Your unconscious memory of previous attempts to speak up causes emotion-related brain areas to trigger the observed physiological response (e.g., desire to vomit, sweating, light-headedness). So, based upon the example above, several pieces of information must be identified during Adaptive Therapy to ask the right question, allowing a drill-down to the core belief "I must be quiet."

- The current event that is causing cognitive dissonance (being asked to stand up and speak to the group).
- The negative feeling that bubbles up (feeling terrified).
- The question is posed to the client: "Why do you feel terrified when asked to speak in front of the group?"
- In this example, the perception is, "I must be quiet."

Just like in a computer, human programming is there to direct tasks in a specific way. While a computer can't violate its programming, a human can. However, once a violation occurs, human programming uses cognitive dissonance to compel conformity once again. In the example above about public speaking, the response could be a shaking of the head and possibly murmuring, "I can't." In an hour or two, cognitive resonance will return as stress hormones are resolved biologically and the feeling of being terrified drops back into the unconscious world it resides in. This unconscious world is attached to public speaking and most probably a number of other events, perceptions, and core beliefs.

If you retain faulty perceptions throughout life, when you interact with the world you will inevitably violate these perceptions, thus producing symptoms. A symptom could be pain, an ache, or exhaustion, even eventually pathology or an unwanted emotional state. Therefore, it only makes sense to identify and modify any beliefs that result in cognitive dissonance. Even if you conform well to your programming, some of these perceptions will result in a difficulty or inability to leverage your talents, develop a purpose in life, or even benefit from good luck coming your way.

AT has long been used in a spiritual psychotherapy model. In spiritual psychotherapy, the self is recognized and seen as the real beingness of an individual, in contrast to the personality being seen as the person's identity, as in some traditional psychological perspectives (Hofmann & Asmundson, 2008). AT recognizes the personality as a collection of perceptions and core beliefs that lead to "labeling," which is found to be self-limiting (Aldao & Nolen-Hoeksema, 2012). Anyone can modify the perceptions that create their self-assigned identity to generate a positive outcome, independent of personality.

The Tools and Techniques of Adaptive Therapy

Evidence-based research is underway for those that lean toward scientific validation of AT. Muscle testing (applied kinesiology) is a subjective tool used by a number of integrative medicine therapists to access client-knowing in the unconscious mind (Slonim, 2012; Hawkins, 2012). Adaptive Therapy has also utilized muscle testing to access the client's unconscious knowing. Therapists ask questions and clients answer verbally what they think is true consciously, followed by the testing of a muscle (e.g., extending the arm, testing the deltoid muscle) to determine if the answer is valid or not. Clients will test "weak" when they cannot resist downward pressure on the arm, indicating that they do not believe the answer to be true. Muscle testing is being replaced with EEG technology that validates or refutes the answer by measuring and interpreting brain waves.

With new technologies, Adaptive Therapy practitioners are developing an evidence-based device to replace muscle testing called "Third-I." Not only will it increase therapists' and clients' trust in the process, but it will also remove the bias that could creep in if the therapist has not personally addressed the client's issue. This device includes a simple brain wave measurement tool (EEG) for use during the line of questioning process taught in AT. This device provides electronic data to indicate whether a statement or answer by the client is true or false, exactly the way muscle testing is used.

Research has already revealed that both positive and negative emotions resonate uniquely in brain wave patterns. For instance, the Scale of Positive and Negative Experience (SPANE) assesses the frequency of positive and negative emotions. It consists of two subscales, one for positive and one for negative effects, with six adjectives each, and measures a broad spectrum of emotions. Scientific studies have demonstrated the good psychometric properties and convergent validity of Third-I technology (Rahm et al., 2017).

This Third-I device is expected to become an FDA-approved medical device for therapists (non-consumer). Adopting this device assists therapists and life coaches in order to augment sessions with clients, increasing efficacy while allowing them to see more clients. Adaptive Therapy does not require nor recommend a weekly appointment, but instead recommends having a new program to work on about every three weeks.

Once a therapist or coach identifies a perception that is self-limiting or causes pain (emotional or physical) in order to modify it, affirmations are used to de-program and re-program that perception. Underlying perceptions are the core issues that form a person's identity, which people create about themselves, others, the world, and others' views of them. Individuals generate perceptions of events to create a protective response against future similar situations, which they have adopted from emotionally charged situations, traumas, and injuries.

Individuals can develop perceptions vicariously by viewing someone else in a situation that the person identifies with. Upon seeing the results of the other's experience, the person comes to believe those results will be true for them as well; for example, the childhood observation "There is never enough money" may be internalized and become the reality of the child, whose experience as an adult repeatedly supports the internal belief that there is not enough money. Even if the adult earns a lot of money, they may find that it always slips away. Even though children act out the parents' beliefs in their own lives, they may be completely unaware that they are doing so.

Some stored perceptions originated as symbols, images, and feelings, and as people mature, they put words to them. For most, when these perceptions are not conformed to, they make themselves known through feelings. Many of the uncomfortable feelings people have in the present are not associated with what is currently happening; they are often responses to an event from the past. The feelings created as a result of perceptions are felt either consciously or expressed in the form of pain or discomfort. In fact, most pain or discomfort (apart from injury) is the result of triggered emotions. This unconscious expression through the physical body is but one way that negative emotions are expressed.

Once the individual acknowledges negative feelings consciously, often the physical pain or discomfort ceases. Then, once conscious, these negative feelings can be examined to determine what perception is being violated. It is interesting to note that many clients of Adaptive Therapy experience pain or discomfort a day or two before an upcoming session; this happens to bring the work to be done during the session to an acute state. For this reason, it is important to address emotional sources of physical pain if there is no pathology. Pain is the body's way to signal the need to address a perception that, when not conformed to, causes discomfort.

It is not the goal of Adaptive Therapy to erase negative feelings. The goal, however, is to use these feelings in a productive way to access the underlying perceptions and core issues in the unconscious that are being violated. Accessing the underlying perceptions offers an opportunity to change these perceptions, thus removing the reason for the negative feelings. Negative feelings attempt to communicate at a conscious level what perceptions are being violated, causing dissonance.

What causes dissonance? One way to understand dissonance is to observe its opposite polarity: resonance. When humans conform to their programming, they experience resonance, which means synchronous vibration. It's also harmony and homeostasis. When humans violate or do not conform to their programming, they experience dissonance, which means discord, conflict, tension, or clash.

Resonance supports health and well-being. Dissonance causes stress, which is a term that covers many different scenarios, but basically means to be out of balance or unwell.

Take a moment to study Diagram 1. According to the Adaptive Therapy philosophy, the system is quite simple. Humans have positive emotions and negative emotions. They also have perceptions that, when conformed to, produce positive feelings which result in cognitive resonance. When a perception is violated, or not conformed to, it generates a negative feeling that bubbles up to consciousness and results in cognitive dissonance. Finally, people have both positive and negative behaviors that are driven by both negative feelings and cognitive dissonance, which pushes behaviors and feelings back into conformity. This is systematic and repeatable all day long as we go about our lives.

Now, you might want to go back and read that again because this is how we, as humans, operate. To be frank, we do not have much control over our emotions, thoughts, or behaviors. It's only when we modify our perceptions and core issues that don't serve us that we can feel a high level of well-being.

The perceptions and core issues logged as "programs" in the unconscious were originally stored there for a good reason—survival. They were placed there to protect the conscious self, to direct the individual to avoid threatening experiences in the present that are similar to a past harmful and painful experience. These programs are also there to reduce stress by providing a blueprint of a past experience which gives a convenient, immediate plan of action for responding to a similar situation in the present. These programs allow people to unconsciously do a task or respond in a situation without thinking because they are operating on automatic pilot. This automatic response is fine as long as the programming serves the host. However, the imperfect physical and emotional health of most people illustrates that they have filed away beliefs that actually create more stress and pain in the present. This programming easily propagates unhealthy lifestyles.

The Role of the Therapist in Adaptive Therapy

From the Adaptive Therapy perspective, a therapist is a vehicle of service that coaches clients in finding and living their purpose. Adaptive therapists don't treat, diagnose, or prescribe but rather listen, reflect, and help clients to explore their inner world. Once a client understands that their programming is the result of exterior forces they responded to for protection (at the time of the original event), it's quite a positive experience for them. Clients then become self-investigators in partnership with their therapist in a safe, inquisitive, and dynamic session.

In order to better help their clients, Adaptive Therapists also work on addressing their own past experiences and how these affect their current emotional state and behavior. These therapists and coaches also learn to examine their own perceptions by listening to emotions that bubble up and then drill down to find the origin of the perception. In some forms of therapy, this is called "pulling the red thread." It is very difficult to help a client with an issue that is also active within the therapist.

In Adaptive Therapy, people have the responsibility to decide if and when they are going to take the steps necessary to heal. If the therapist pushes clients or reveals information before it is appropriate, it slows down their healing process and can actually cause more pain or acuteness of a symptom. Therapists should seek permission before asking any questions that will reveal an individual's unconscious agendas. Therefore, Adaptive Therapists are careful to investigate only subjects that the client's inner wisdom has directed them to explore.

Adaptive Therapy is not about positioning therapists as the expert with techniques and information to direct clients in their healing; instead, it is about being present for clients so they may direct their own healing. Adaptive Therapy empowers the client. Adaptive Therapy is a service.

Some key principles of Adaptive Therapy:

1. People don't intentionally do anyone harm; they react from programming ("It's okay to steal to survive").

2. If someone does cause harm to another, he/she is following his/her programming ("I have to stop a competitor before they beat me").

3. When faced with a new event, people react more primitively (hoarding toilet paper during the Covid pandemic).

4. People catalog an emotional event for use in a similar situation in the future to provide an instinctive response that is rapid (and known to have worked correctly in the past to provide protection). This is also more efficient, direct, and specific than just the "fight or flight" syndrome.

5. Adaptive Therapists embrace the use of 500 emotions called "feeling flavors" that help to define the core issue. If the therapist identifies the exact feeling with the client, it is easier to identify the core belief underlying the feeling. For example, anger is inclusive of many emotional flavors. However, feeling defiant is more revealing (i.e. "Why did you feel defiant when you found out someone talked behind your back?") A general feeling of anger would not easily point to a core issue such as "I always get even."

6. What people hate in others triggers something within them. A negative emotion is bubbling up in them, causing them to experience feelings triggered by someone

else's behavior. If they didn't have the emotion within themselves, they would not be triggered.

7. What people admire in others is a reflection of who they are or could be.

8. When addressing an issue, Adaptive Therapists re-program both perceptions and core issues to eradicate behavior quickly and permanently. An example of re-programming a perception (addressing the behavioral aspect) would be using the affirmation "I no longer feel that people cut me off while driving." The core issue could be "I must be first," and re-programming would shift that to sharing the space with others, such as a belief that "People know to give me leeway in traffic."

9. The process includes asking why, so the client can identify the original recording of the perception or core belief. The therapist typically repeats the question a number of times, such as "Why do you feel defiant when someone talks behind your back?" Then the therapist asks the client to think back to a time in the past when this happened.

10. Muscle testing is used only to verify the validity of a client's conscious answer, in search of unbeneficial perceptions and core issues.

11. It's helpful if a therapist is in a state of perpetual wonder, asking questions of themselves and their clients without expectation.

12. In addition to modifying core issues, there are advanced techniques to specifically address post-traumatic stress disorder (PTSD), phobias, co-dependency, conflicts of will, time disorders, temperaments, black holes (a process for alleviating projection on others as an adult for unmet childhood needs such as neglect, abuse, loss), attitudes, view of life, drivers, addiction, denial, bias, definitions, and traumas.

13. No one does anything "to us," but people do things "for us," which means anyone triggering clients is trying to help them become aware of an issue that is limiting or hurting their life.

14. Formation of the original core belief process:

    a. An emotionally charged experience: Mom puts her 3-year-old child's hand on a hot burner to teach her not to play with the knobs on the stove. Of course, this is abuse but it really happened to a client, so it is based on a lived experience.

    b. Emotion: The mother is feeling at wit's end, which leads her to make a decision that could harm her child. (The mother's emotion is adopted by the child and tagged to the event).

    c. Core belief established: "I never learn."

    d. And then future events that trigger the encoded experience:

        i. Experience: Any learning experiences, such as attending school or learning to ride a bike.

ii. Emotion: Feeling "at wit's end" (similar to how her mother felt).

iii. Core belief: "I never learn," which causes lack of interest in learning, daydreaming, avoiding school, failure behavior, dropping out; this belief creates the inability to concentrate, due to the stressor of feeling "at wit's end."

Adaptive Therapy does not seek to address a diagnosis that someone may wish to pursue. However, oftentimes clients will indicate a medical issue that they want to understand and learn how they might be contributing emotionally to its presence, and Adaptive Therapists will oblige. Performance enhancement is also an area in which Adaptive Therapy is useful by helping to connect clients to their inner beliefs about a sport and disconnect any emotional triggers that might bubble up during play. And finally, Adaptive Therapy is for anyone looking for hope, vision, and purpose.

Maslow's Hierarchy of Needs conveys the journey all humans undertake to fulfill their desire to live life fully. However, most people feel blocked, living well below Self-actualization as they scratch for necessities such as food, rent, and childcare while working several jobs. No wonder hope is lost. And with the pro-consumerism mantra, life feels even emptier as most people go without. Is it any wonder people are looking for and latching onto anything that can offer hope?

Adaptive Therapy offers hope. It is a way to experience a purpose-filled life on the inside, and to manifest it on the outside by modifying core beliefs. It's not about programming yourself for success, riches, and material possessions. Adaptive Therapy is really about modifying programming that compels you to do things you really don't *want* to do and to want things you really don't need. Remember, marketing and advertising has the capability to program you too (Gangadharbatla & Daugherty, 2013; Sarar, 2016; Ardiansyah & Sarwoko, 2020; Ioanas & Stoica, 2020).

Adaptive Therapy helps anyone who feels left out and helps people realize their ultimate goal without feeling limited by any external circumstance. When people are whole and healthy within, they are whole and healthy walking through their life, interacting with others, and becoming a contributor to solutions. This is what it means to live a life with purpose.

Visit https://IAffirm.org to find an Adaptive Therapy Therapist.

References

Aldao, A, Nolen-Hoeksema, S. (2012). "When are adaptive strategies most predictive of psychopathology?" *Journal of Abnormal Psychology, 121*(1), 276–281.

Ardiansyah, F, Sarwoko, E. (2020). "How social media marketing influences consumers' purchase decision? A mediation analysis of brand awareness." *JEMA, 17*(2), 156-168.

Beck, JS. (1964). *Cognitive therapy: basics and beyond.* New York. Guildford Press.

Beck, AT. (1976). *Cognitive therapy and the emotional disorders.* New York, NY. International Universities Press.

Beck, AT, Rush, J, Shaw, B, Emery, G. (1979). *Cognitive therapy of depression.* New York. Guildford Press.

Craske, MG. (2010). *Cognitive–behavioral therapy.* American Psychological Association.

Eels, T. (1997). *Handbook of psychotherapy case formulation.* New York. Guilford Press.

Gangadharbatla, H, Daugherty, T. (2013). "Advertising versus product placements: how consumers assess the value of each." *Journal of Current Issues & Research in Advertising, 34,* 21–38.

Greenberger, D, Padesky, C. (1995). *Mind over mood: A cognitive therapy treatment manual for clients.* New York. Guilford Press.

Hawkins, D. (2012). *Power vs. force: The hidden determinants of human behavior.* Hay House Publishing Group.

Hofmann, SG, Asmundson, GJG. (2008). "Acceptance and mindfulness-based therapy: New wave or old hat?" *Clinical Psychology Review, 28*(1), 1-16.

Ioanas, E, Stoica, I. (2020). "Social media and its impact on consumers' behavior." *International Journal of Economic Practices and Theories, 4*(2), 295-303.

Rahm T, Heise E, Schuldt, M. (2017). *Measuring the frequency of emotions—validation of the Scale of Positive and Negative Experience (SPANE) in Germany. PLoS One, 12*(2), e0171288.

Sarar, H. (2016). "Consumers Responses to traditional and non-traditional advertisements." *Advances in Social Sciences Research Journal, 3*(6), 192-205.

Slonim, D. (2012). *Applied kinesiology as a tool to bring a paradigm shift in psychology.* Association for Comprehensive Energy Psychology.

CHAPTER 2

Foundation of Adaptive Therapy

Adaptive Therapy was founded upon the groundwork laid out by Biokinesiology, EduKinesiology, and Touch for Health. All these practices use applied kinesiology as an investigative tool to determine where imbalances in the body/mind may lie.

John Barton founded Biokinesiology, a process of mapping the specific emotions that have either a positive or negative effect on the integrity of muscles, tendons, ligaments, and fascia; the function of organs and glands; and the various energy centers in the body. Barton discovered the link between emotions and energetic imbalances in the body that, in turn, produce physical symptoms. While Barton was a pioneer working with thousands of people with anecdotal success, recent research reveals the connection between stress and disease (Sapolsky, 2007; Cohen et al, 2016). Stress is simply a term that is better stated as stressors, such as criticism, pressure, or gossip. In Adaptive Therapy, therapists help to increase self-esteem so that previously experienced stressors no longer impact a person in the same way. After all, some people do not view criticism as a stressful experience, but instead as a learning experience which is not a stressor. Paul Dennison founded EduKinesiology, which is devoted to the improvement of learning, especially for people with learning disabilities. Finally, John Thie, a chiropractor, developed Touch for Health, a process used to discover imbalance and corrections to spinal alignment.

Similarly, Adaptive Therapy allows us to learn about our reactions to stressors by examining our current emotional response to stored perceptions in our unconscious that are activated by present events. Adaptive Therapy is a tool that helps us access our inner knowing to heal through a process of removing, replacing, and reprogramming belief systems and core issues, thus modifying behavior.

Conformity

Any typical family believes it is their responsibility to shape the minds of their young, using punishment or reward to achieve conformity. But conformity to what? Usually, it is conformity to a family system with roles and rules which do not fit or support the individuality within each child. In fact, our programming from childhood can be extremely detrimental to living a full life, since our purpose is veiled in a cloud. The manifestation of our past programming in the present blocks our conscious awareness of how we could contribute to the

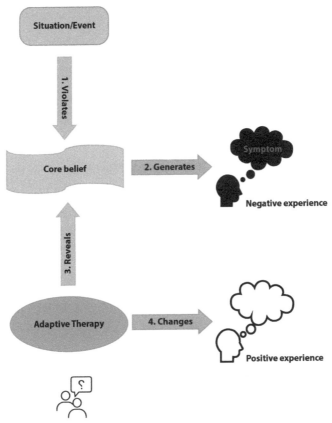

The therapists asks the subject:
"Why do you feel the negative emotion when the situation/event occurs?"

good of the world and become the leader we innately are. It may repress any drive to achieve at all.

For most, our innate uniqueness becomes inaccessible; our conscious self-claims its position as who we are, and our True Self is repressed into silence. No wonder people are confused and asking "What is my purpose? Who am I? Why are we here?" I don't claim to know the answers, but I do live a life that feels aligned with the "Who" I have discovered from about 10 years old to today. In fact, if you want a glimpse of who you really are, ask your parents about you as a child under five years old. "How did I behave?" I know for me, I would say, "Look at what I can do!" My parents said I was "full of myself," and they had to ignore me so that I would not get "a big head." Imagine how much work it took to discover who I was. My parents ignored who I *really* was and never validated it. When children receive this type of messaging, it cuts off their awareness of the True Self.

So, what is to be done? Do we let our children grow up wild? No, because that is going to the opposite extreme of neglect. A good parent is one who nurtures a child's individuality while teaching principles, culture, and self-awareness. This nurturing approach will yield a child that goes on to great success.

It may be difficult to understand or appreciate the significance and the far-reaching consequences of thinking that the True Self is the conscious self. Many are unaware of the unconscious self, thinking that only their conscience tells them what is right or wrong. There is another part of the Self in the unconscious state that wants to reveal itself but has very limited expression because of the human constraint of conformity. Humans are programmed to follow their core beliefs and respond by acting upon perceptions. When core beliefs are deviated from, individuals experience emotional and/or physical pain to push them back to their programming. Conformity is the rule that hides the True Self from consciousness.

True Self

So, what is this True Self? Is it spiritual or is it just the mind? After working with thousands of clients, my answer is that it can be both or either, depending upon the belief system of the client. In fact, the answer doesn't really matter because what people believe drives them toward achieving their full potential. Myself, I prefer to believe that the brain is programmed like a computer with a unique mind that strives for Self-actualization. The mind gives us the ability to be aware of our best interests. I also believe that the mind is the director of ourselves; if we let it, it supports our growth to our fullest potential. This programming established in the brain contains the obstacles we need to overcome for achieving greatness. My intention is to confirm this idea by actively conducting research in my nonprofit organization IAffirm (https://IAffirm.org).

I also believe that alternative health practitioners have been more likely to discover the role of the mind because science relies on quantifiable data; since the True Self (Mind) is intangible, it has not been possible to prove the role of the mind. However, new technologies can do this, and validation can be expected in the future. An example of advances in understanding language and the brain was found using neuroprosthesis, combined with new deep learning algorithms. This combination has enabled scientists to access the brain waves of a man unable to speak due to severe paralysis by transforming his thoughts into sentences (Moses et al., 2021). This is only the beginning.

Many people believe their personalities are their actual self, or that what they do is who they are. They have no context for comparing the experience of the personality with the uniqueness that has been lost. From this perspective, reclaiming their True Self seems almost impossible, especially when they may not be aware of their uniqueness. They are robotized, responding to their environment based on past experiences. However, if they choose to explore the possibility of self-renewal, they can in fact begin to access and live from their uniqueness, their True Self. They need to de-identify with their personality and how they perform, their sense of ego identity, and become aware of the True Self.

Personally, I am always on this journey. I understand much about myself starting with being the daughter of a nuclear physicist and a religious devotee. As a result, I have a huge comfort zone. I grew up confident in myself, learned about trees and plants from arboretum classes and won a swimming contest early on. My parents' divorce when I was 12 shaped me, as well as being under the roof of strict religious discipline throughout my teenage years. My best subjects in school were art, typing, and writing. This explains my high interest in graphic design, video production, writing books, teaching, and video software development. My path led me ultimately to work in therapy with clients. It was my natural proclivity and path of least resistance. But these talents and experiences are still leading to so much more, as you will see in my work as the founder of Adaptive Therapy and the software I am developing that mirrors this process, which, when adapted to scale, will help millions.

As previously discussed, in Adaptive Therapy people extract old beliefs and replace them with new ones that are in alignment with their True Self. This True Self is the director of our lives and if we follow it, we can remove the blocks in our programmed brain and achieve our full potential.

At some point in our personal growth there is a shift in operation, from the conscious self to the True Self. The conscious self then serves the True Self, having recognized that the process of being directed by the True Self has more benefit for the overall survival and health of the host (person). This shift, however, does not mean that things are now going to run perfectly. Instead, a new process has begun to maintain the commitment to identify and rework any issue that distorts the expression of the True Self. People will always have new experiences that trigger different and deeper past perceptions that affect behavior. Removing blocks and keeping clear are lifelong tasks. Prior to this shift, the True Self was covered and mute. The shift now opens the door for its expression. And the True Self has a big job to do, mediating all the aspects of the Self into an organized, collaborative symphony for pure expression. As anyone applying Adaptive Therapy techniques will tell you, the process never ends. However, at this point, the journey is empowering, intriguing, and fun.

Conscience

In Adaptive Therapy we view the conscience as a part of our consciousness, guiding us to make decisions based upon what we know is right or wrong. Animals also have a conscience; hence they can demonstrate emotions of shame and exhibit behavior that acknowledges they know they have done something wrong. I have never worked with anyone without a conscience, but I am sure, based upon others who have, there are some people that don't, or it's disengaged. The lack of conscience allows the person to do whatever they will.

So, if the conscience is the arbitrator of what is right or wrong, then how do we square someone killing purposefully? This person may know killing is wrong in their conscience, but they feel helpful when they kill someone they determine to be a bad person. They are just fulfilling their belief system: "It's my job to kill bad people." And when they see but don't kill a bad person, they experience negative feelings that force them into compliance, into conformity with core beliefs; thus they are compelled to kill. Serial killers deal with this compulsion and usually come from a family where someone was abused, and they couldn't save them (including themselves). In this example, negative feelings would be the opposite of helpful, since they would feel "too impotent to help." This is an extreme example, but if a serial killer can kill and feel good about it, then imagine the person who can justify cheating at a game when programmed to think, "You are a loser if you don't always win."

So, the conscience is above the unconscious state and below consciousness until triggered by a choice someone is contemplating or about to act upon. The conscience, while a powerful guide to our behavior, is not in control of emotions, belief systems, or our behavior. It only provides guidance, and in Adaptive Therapy, it acts as a filter to modify the intensity of expression. For example, a driver cuts a person off in traffic, who then flips the driver off while cursing. Someone else might honk the horn while another steps on the brakes. Why do different people respond differently to the same situation? Their programming and their conscience filter the response caused by their belief system. Suppose that the three people in the example above hold these different beliefs:

1. "I have the right to hit back."
2. "I have the right to push back."
3. "I don't sweat the small stuff."

Each person in this example knows in their conscience it's wrong to respond negatively. The first person will push their conscience aside and respond at "10 intensity." The person honking responds with "4 or 5 intensity," while the person who steps on the brake for safety is not reacting negatively at all. In our work, Adaptive Therapists view the conscience as not having the ability to circumvent any automatic response from programming; the conscience only has the ability to temper it (Kissin, 1986; Bleichmar, 2004).

The Conscious Mind

Without much difficulty, most people can describe what is conscious to them, what they are aware of. Awareness can start with the senses, in what people can hear, smell, taste, touch, and see on demand without thinking. The body also modulates all the systems that people consciously know are working, including temperature control, breathing, and heartbeat, and the chemistry that underlies them. The mind then is conscious of walking through a room, maybe noting something out of place or new; if the temperature changes too much, a behavioral urge occurs to check the thermometer in the room. Then there are "thoughts" that can come from nowhere or that people catch themselves ruminating about. Many people with schedules are aware of what they need to be doing most of the time. Others who are at work are aware of having tasks to do. People drive to and from work or walk to mass transit all the while thinking about things. This is what people call consciousness, for the most part.

There is another part of awareness that can become conscious, but not all the time. For example, you "know" your favorite things, like colors, car brand, a trip you went on, or certain childhood memories. However, you are not always conscious of this information. If you were, you would be inundated with too much information to keep in conscious awareness, and your mind would attempt to push it back into unconsciousness. But no one has to do that because humans have a nicely lubricated system of thoughts slipping in and out of consciousness on demand.

This explains how the conscious mind works as designed and evolved. The mind can also be aware of pain when stubbing a toe or falling. When recalling to consciousness the death of a loved one, a person can also feel emotional pain, which then produces behavior such as crying.

The conscious mind is innately positive. This explains how tasks can be accomplished without emotional interference, which happens to be more innately negative.

Most psychologists agree that there is a conscious top-level emotional experience that consists of about six universal emotions: happiness, sadness, disgust, fear, surprise, and anger (Ekman, 1999; Sauter et al., 2010). However, the unconscious mind tags specifically to an emotion, probably for protection. Protection from what, though? Considering that humans are geared for safety first, to survive and propagate, it appears necessary to withhold specific emotions from automatic conscious release, in order to keep the wraps tight on core beliefs established earlier that are connected to safety. Remember, Adaptive Therapy seeks to identify the specific emotion tied to an event in order to know the developed perception from replications of the event, and also to change the core belief.

Detailing the conscious mind helps people understand when and why emotions enter consciousness, specifically negative ones. Paying attention to these emotions reveals what core issue is being triggered. These core issues, once faced and processed, lead to fewer negative emotions bubbling up automatically.

The conscious mind also solves problems, weighs pros and cons, and makes decisions based upon analysis. Core issues can influence all of these functions, which becomes apparent when emotions are triggered. For example, a discussion of facts might quickly elevate into conflict when disagreement occurs. Passion levels rise when emotions assert themselves, revealing what each side believes—their core issues.

The Unconscious Mind

The unconscious mind is the database of our lives. Its purpose is to pay attention to what is happening below consciousness for cues to respond. Responses include protection, procreation opportunities, and ways to be more efficient by automating repetitive tasks like walking, recognizing someone, or driving. This explains why humans are often defensive, seek partners for procreation, and like to multi-task. This has worked for millennia. In earlier times most people did not need a professional therapist because they consulted family members, a teacher, clergy, and occasionally a counselor. Therapists were seen as those one went to with a "mental disorder," not stress, physical pain, or illness. Short of a diagnosed mental disorder, most people have coped well with the ups and downs of life. This also explains why people don't want to go to a therapist because of this stigma; going to one may earn you the label "crazy." It probably also triggers experiences from elementary and middle school, where less-abled students were socially rejected.

In the modern world, something has radically changed. People are not coping well anymore. Why? Human consciousness was not configured to be constantly bombarded by emotions, to juggle many activities simultaneously, or be impacted by continual traumas like Covid-19, extreme weather events, news stories on mass shootings, political rivalries, or other disasters. The unconscious mind was not designed to function continuously dealing with multiple issues that are often conflicting and that disrupt efficiency, one of the core competencies of the unconscious! Recent research supports this idea, noting that understanding and experience are combined in a way that allows people to figure things out, i.e., it is not just a mental activity (Gray, 1999; Unkelbach & Greifeneder, 2013).

Dealing with multiple issues causes a perpetual state of cognitive dissonance, because humans are not good at change and, in fact, they dislike it. Computer software gets updates. humans also get updates, through experience, changing perceptions, and altering core beliefs, but only after deep learning through trust, emotional processing, and repetition.

Life is so much easier when one doesn't have to think about how to do something that has been done many times before. Things can just happen automatically, from rote memory. The heart doesn't need to be told to beat and people don't need to tell the body to stand, walk, or run. As a result, the unconscious mind takes these functions over so the conscious mind can focus on more important matters.

What shapes the unconscious mind? Parents, caregivers, educators, social media, advertisements, ministers, and other "trusted" leaders. Trust is the common denominator of these influencers. In addition to trust, emotion is also a requirement to encode perceptions and core beliefs. While emotion is not typically viewed as a "sense," it performs like one, eliciting data when experienced (Ford & Gross, 2018). Another requirement is repetition. And finally, a cognitive assessment occurs to evaluate the consequences of adoption: "Will I still belong to my 'personal community' if I do?" It's disconcerting how easy it is to "get programmed." The effects of programming show why it's so easy to lose touch with the True Self. Before children are even on their own, they are set up to live a life based on where they grew up, how they grew up, who taught them, who cared for them, how much "programming" they absorbed, and what their economic condition was.

In childhood, the unconscious is only equipped with basic fight or flight responses and genetic memories to keep the host safe. A great deal of the child's activity is automatic, probably because it's part of the autonomic nervous system (Kiefer, 2007). As children grow to adulthood, through experience they develop enhanced protective measures, learn to be efficient as tasks are mastered, and become aware of their sexual drive.

It will be helpful to walk through an encoding experience to understand how this works:

A baby is on a changing table with their diaper ready to be removed when Mom remembers she forgot to grab the new wipes she just bought. She steps out and upon her return and, to her horror, the baby is now upside down in the waste basket, not crying. Mom quickly grabs the child, completely freaked out, and cuddles the baby while checking for injuries.

The baby now cries because Mom is very upset, terrified she has hurt her child.

So, what is the baby's perception of this experience? The baby has no words, only the feeling of falling, landing on its head, and possibly suffocating in a basket for 30 seconds. Then came Mom's reaction of terror. Remember, encoding takes four elements: trust, emotion, repetition, and being accepted by one's tribe.

Mom is trusted, check. Mom is emoting, check. Repetition? Not yet, but later in life when a similar event occurs, this memory will be triggered and the new event will join this event to reinforce its effects.

The encoding process will include the event, which is falling, landing upside down, and hitting the head. The emotion is terror and the perception is most probably, "I'm going to get hurt if I fall" or "I'm going to die if I fall," since Mom is projecting fear that her child's neck might be broken. While the child does not have language to formulate an actual perception or core issue, the message is clear: the "falling feeling" is deadly and precautions against falling should be at the top of the mind.

A few years later a trip to the local county fair offers a ride that the child is excited to get on. Mom is at the child's side, and the ride starts. As soon as the child feels the "falling feeling," it freaks out and wants to get off. Mom gets upset, terrified in fact, because her child is trying to wriggle out of the seat to get off immediately. Reinforcement occurs in this situation, but this time there are words attached to the event, both the past and the present. Note that experiences encoded with emotion, perception, and core belief are not organized by date or time (Pally, 2007; Erskine, 2010). But this time the words are clear: "I'm going to die if I fall." This belief does not serve the child and will not in the future; for instance, they might respond similarly if there is turbulence during a flight, when skiing down a hill, or driving near the edge of a road on a ravine. Holding this core belief will cause recurrent debilitation; it needs modification through therapy to develop a belief such as, "I'm safe, even if I fall."

Reinforcement occurs over and over again, each time an event similar to what is encoded happens, adding additional perceptions to the reason why the event must be avoided at all costs. Even thinking about going on a plane will be a trigger, since turbulence could cause the plane to fall, and death will be the end result. What's so difficult about identifying and changing these beliefs is that the original event itself does not become conscious, only the feeling of terror when faced with a similar event. This is why Adaptive Therapy emphasizes paying attention to the feelings that bubble up, the inner voice of the unconscious speaking, giving hints about the programming that is self-limiting and often self-harming.

Perceptions

Perceptions are the result of a cognitive assessment of data to compare, correlate, and predict situations at the unconscious level to avoid disturbing conscious activity. An example of this is a familiar one: discrepancy in expected weight or distance. Remember the last time you went to pick up a grocery bag or step down some stairs, expecting a certain amount of weight or distance, but to your surprise the expectation was not accurate? This occurs because your body functions based upon an assumption as a result of a perception, such as: "groceries weigh an average of X," so the amount of effort to pick them up was calculated for the current bag. If, however, the grocery bag holds feathers or multiple cans of soup, the surprise you feel is the result of a deviation from the perception. The stairs dropping lower than expected could be the result of a steeper decline from an attic room and dim light that did not allow assessment in real-time. Perceptions are used to speed reaction time for safety and efficiency.

Some perceptions are faulty and can even be deadly. In my almost 40 years of work with clients, a particular example comes to mind involving driving. A woman turned left from a driveway onto the road, stopped, looked, and then proceeded. She did not see the motorcycle she cut off, which resulted in a crash, causing his demise. Why did this happen? This woman had never experienced seeing a motorcycle driving in the lane where she was turning, so her lack of experience, a memory to recall, or a warning of danger, allowed her to move forward. This explains why experiencing different situations and learning widely will improve perception. Teaching children they have permission to say "No" to a stranger and run is protecting children. If parents don't do this, children have no previous threatening experience to guard against and their innocence can be robbed too early in life.

Since there can be risk of life and limb when operating from perceptions surrounding core issues, should people do more thinking instead? Not really. It's not efficient and could actually lead to more harm. Thinking what to do to react to danger is slower than reacting from perception. The best sports performers are those that do not analyze their reactions, but rely on their learned ones, improving over time and repetition (Hannin et al., 2002). The same holds true in a car accident that is unfolding, a fall, or performing on an exam.

Personal Examples of the Benefits of Perception:

I had a fall while hiking and I only remember the misstep, then I blacked out. I became conscious again, probably only seconds later, as I hit the ground, back arched to avoid the rock just under my face, hands under my chest to protect it, and a perfect plant with no skidding or rolling, that fractured my wrist. I realized immediately that I was not okay and wailed for a bit. However, it's amazing that I was not killed, because I was on a rock fall that had multiple rocks. I was facing uphill, so I was at risk of falling backwards and breaking my back or hitting my head. I apparently pivoted to face downhill and dove for the only safe spot between rocks, about six feet lower than where I had been standing. So, what happened? My unconscious mind took over and shut my conscious mind out from any interference, determining that I was at risk of dying. This is why I have no conscious memory of the dive; I was checked out. Have I fallen before? Yes. I fell in a cave once, slipping on the moss-covered rock stairs and I can recall this fall. My arms dropped down to my sides and my palms caught my weight. I was also aware of my legs tucking up in the air to avoid direct tailbone impact with the stairs. As a result, I reinforced my perceptions, "I'm going to die if I fall," and my unconscious "rescue mode" took over.

I had also seen my friend ride her bike down a hill that was too much for her. She went over the handlebars and was badly skinned up, so a new perception was developed, "I don't ride down hills on bikes, period!"

I also fell in the bathtub, but again while the fall was bad and I broke my cheekbone, it was the perfect fall based upon physics. My cheekbone hit the toilet bowl and broke the seat. This event added to my encoding with regard to falling: "I'm not safe in the shower either." My unconscious does all it can to protect me from the danger of falling. After all, I was the child on the changing table that fell head-first into the waste basket.

Core Identity

How is a core identity different than a perception? In my experience with clients, a perception is a way to react, to respond automatically in a given situation for the purpose of safety and/or efficiency. Core Identity is the result of the response that can be identified by asking the question, "Why?"; "Why did I respond that way?" It's the process of how one identifies with the self.

In Cognitive Behavioral Therapy, core beliefs (which Adaptive Therapy calls core identity) are viewed as a person's most central ideas about themselves, others, and the world (Wenzel, 2012). Adaptive Therapy agrees but adds a dimension about how people believe others view them. For Adaptive Therapists, it's highly important to recognize and reprogram how people think of these core beliefs.

Let's look at an example of the relationship between a perception and a core belief. A man is grumpy and "pissed off" when things don't work as advertised, a bottom sheet won't easily go on his bed, or a light bulb keeps burning out too soon. The man's emotion triggered during these events (small, but petty irritants in life) was one of being worthless. The perception was that that "Things don't work like they should." Walking around with this perception will magnify the problem, so changing this perception is recommended.

But what is the core issue here? In this case, it's about being a perfectionist, a requirement spread across his world to avoid feeling worthless. After all, worthless things are a reflection of this man when he couldn't be perfect. In therapy, this grumpy person can modify the core issue from "I must be a perfectionist" to being an idealist instead. Perhaps this client could have chosen to be a realist instead, but his choice was to be an idealist.

So, a perception is an assessment and definition of an external event; and core identity is an internal assessment of self, others, the world, or how others view you.

Multiple Perceptions	Connected to a Core Issue
"A person's GPA defines how smart someone is." "Uneducated people should not have kids." "Uneducated people perpetuate their problems." "Anti-maskers are ignorant." "Anti-vaxxers don't believe in science."	"Higher education is the only equalizer for me or for others."
"Men are only after one thing, watch out!" "I always pick guys that cheat on me."	"Men are predators."
"Politicians divide us on purpose." "Politicians only say what they think others want to hear." "Politicians can't seem to find common ground."	"Politicians are untrustworthy."
"People seem to ignore me most of the time." "I never get calls back after auditions." "I get cut off in traffic all the time."	"No one sees me."

Ego—The Human Need to Be Right

A discussion about Adaptive Therapy would not be complete without covering conflict—with self, others, and the world; this is especially true when observing the world today, that seems to have reached a point of instability, producing new emotional complexity to already frenzied lives.

The ego is associated with personal identity and self-esteem (Lapsley & Power, 1988). As a result, people too often believe they are right about something when they are not. Even if they become aware that they are wrong, most cannot admit it. Why does ego exist? Survival.

Consider people that appear to have poor egos: those that have low self-esteem, are prone to suicide, and use drugs, alcohol, and other distractions to avoid facing what they perceived as facts about themselves: that they are a loser, inadequate, can't do anything right. So they think, "Why try? I'll fail anyway." It seems to make sense that people who always feel right, correct, and are self-absorbed live a better life. But where is the balance? It's not healthy on either side of the equation—too much or too little ego.

Adaptive Therapy identifies the ego as derived from the development of perceptions wherein people believe they are their achievements or failures, the sum of their wins and losses, and their behaviors. This is a faulty belief. Instead, Adaptive Therapists support the belief that "I am not what I do," rather "I am my Being," which is quite a good belief. When a person can identify with Being (their True Self) instead of what they do, then they are not deprecated by admitting a mistake.

The beauty of admitting a mistake is that now there is an opportunity to modify one's behavior, to avoid making a mistake in the future in the same way. Learning can only happen when one admits a mistake and strives to learn as much as possible about it.

So, the real illness going on in today's world is the loss of Self-awareness, mistaking *who* one really is for *what* one does. Self-awareness is not taught or modeled widely. Therefore, it's up to each person to learn it and teach it to the next generation.

The greatest strength comes from knowing that everyone is fallible and that everyone is doing their best; refraining from judging others or oneself in the process is a way of seeking to become conscious of the True Self. In being the True Self, people can contribute positively to others and the world.

Free Will

The concept that humans have free will is not yet agreed upon in the scientific literature. Older schools of thought believe that there is no free will, which means that people have no choice (Sappington, 1990). Adaptive Therapy offers that people do have free will. If they didn't, then people would be just like animals. Adaptive Therapists believe that this differentiation provides humans with awareness and consciousness (Vohs & Schooler, 2008; Baumeister et al., 2010).

Examples of free will are when people contemplate or dream about something, maybe changing a job or moving to another house. The old theories suggest that people do not freely formulate their intent. However, feeling dissatisfaction in a job and knowing there are lots of jobs out there with higher pay does not automatically motivate someone to get a new job. Being exposed to new facts can trigger wonder in someone, who then ponders how this affects them personally and questions whether a change is needed or desired. The brain does not dictate a change in this case, hence free will.

Climate change may cause fear for one's family, so people look into moving to a safer place. One person may hear about a flood tragedy and modify his or her intention to tolerate this and take the risk of living in a flood zone. Another person may respond by moving, while yet another may decide to build resilience in the home. If people do not have free will, then they are just robots with no purpose for existence.

Free will underlies invention and the desire to achieve, albeit motivated by the exhilaration, the high, of looking forward to achievement, or bathing in it when it arrives. Thinking outside the box, pursuing different goals, and challenging the status quo are also examples of free will in action.

Therefore, free will is available to humans to creatively assess and decide an action, either a new one or an improvement to what already is. Scientific research on college students demonstrates that synaptic wiring at a rapid pace is the physical mechanism that gives humans the power to exercise free will (Tse, 2013). It would be interesting to conduct the same synapse study on different types of people, not just college students. Inventors would probably be among those most capable of exercising free will, as well as people that reject the status quo. Then it would be instructive to compare and contrast these subjects with people that are viewed as having "herd mind."

References

Baumeister, RF, Mele, AR, Vohs, KD. (2010). *Free will and consciousness: How might they work?* Oxford University Press. (pp. 1-240).

Bleichmar, H. (2004). Making conscious the unconscious in order to modify unconscious processing: Some mechanisms of therapeutic change. *Int J Psychoanal, 85,* 1379-1400.

Cohen, S, Gianaros, PJ, Manuck, SB. A stage model of stress and disease. (2016). *Perspect Psychol Sci, 11*(4), 456–463.

Ekman, P. Basic emotions. In T. Dalgleish & M. J. Power (Eds.) (1999*). Handbook of cognition and emotion.* John Wiley & Sons Ltd. (pp. 45–60).

Erskine, RG. (2010). Life scripts: Unconscious relational patterns and psychotherapeutic involvement. In R. G. Erskine, *Life scripts: A transactional analysis of unconscious relational patterns.* Karnac Books. (pp. 1–28).

Ford, BQ, Gross, JJ. (2018). Emotion regulation: Why beliefs matter. *Canadian Psychology/Psychologie canadienne, 59*(1), 1–14.

Gray, JA. (1999). Cognition, emotion, conscious experience and the brain. In T. Dalgleish & M. J. Power (Eds.), *Handbook of cognition and emotion.* John Wiley & Sons Ltd. (pp. 83–102).

Hannin, Y, Korjus, T, Jouste, P, Baxter, P. (2002). Rapid technique correction using old way/new way: Two case studies with Olympic athletes. *Human Kinetics J, 16*(1), 79-99.

Kiefer, M. (2007). Top-down modulation of unconscious 'automatic' processes: A gating framework. *Adv Cogn Psychol, 3*(1-2), 289–306.

Kissin, B. Conscious and Unconscious Programs in the Brain. (1986). *Perspective in social psychology.* Springer.

Lapsley, DK, Power, FC. (1988). Self, ego, and identity: Integrative approaches. *Psychology.* Springer. (pp 1-85).

Moses, DA, Metzger, SL, Liu, JR, Anumanchipalli, GK, Makin, JG, Sun, PF, Chartier, J, Dougherty, ME, Liu, PM, Abrams, GM, Tu-Chan, A, Ganguly, K, Chang, EF. (2021). Neuroprosthesis for decoding speech in a paralyzed person with anarthria. *N Engl J Med, 385,* 217-227.

Pally, R. (2007). The predicting brain: Unconscious repetition, conscious reflection and therapeutic change. *Int J Psychoanal, 88*(4), 861-881.

Sapolsky, RM. Stress, Stress-related disease, and emotional regulation. (2007). In J. J. Gross (Ed.), *Handbook of emotion regulation.* The Guilford Press. (pp. 606–615).

Sappington, AA. (1990). Recent psychological approaches to the free will versus determinism issue. *Psychological Bulletin, 108*(1), 19–29.

Sauter, DA, Eisner, F, Ekman, P, Scott, SK. (2010). Cross-cultural recognition of basic emotions through nonverbal emotional vocalizations. *PNAS, 107*(6), 2408-2412.

Tse, P. (2013). *The neural basis of free will: Criterial causation.* MIT Press. (pp 1-456).

Unkelbach, C, Greifeneder R. (2013). *The Experience of thinking how the fluency of mental processes influences cog-*

nition and behaviour. Psychology Press, Taylor & Francis. (pp. 1-288).

Vohs, KD, Schooler, JW. (2008). The value of believing in free will: encouraging a belief in determinism increases cheating. *Psychol Sci Sage J, 19*(1), 49-54.

Wenzel, A. (2012). Modification of core beliefs in cognitive therapy. *Psychology.* Intech. (pp 1-204).

CHAPTER 3

The Techniques of Adaptive Therapy

Applied Kinesiology

Kinesiology is the study of physical activity and muscle movement. It is a discipline studied at many colleges by future physical therapists and other healthcare professionals. The mechanics of applied kinesiology are quite simple, in that muscle movement is used as a diagnostic method. Muscle testing is another way of describing the use of applied kinesiology. In the case of Adaptive Therapy, muscle movement is used to determine where and what psychological imbalances are present.

Adaptive Therapy requires specific ways of using applied kinesiology, much like Touch for Health, Biokinesiology, EduKinesiology, and the manual method used by chiropractors. There are associations within the field of applied kinesiology that divide the various approaches utilizing muscle testing. Those who consider themselves "expert" technicians of kinesiology are professionals with many years of formal education, who have added the techniques of applied kinesiology to their primary practice. They believe "their way" is more credible than any other and by proclamation have said others using "their tool" cannot call it what they do—applied kinesiology. However, Adaptive Therapy uses applied kinesiology/muscle testing as its investigative tool and teaches practitioners to use it with integrity. Calling the tool by any other name would be misleading.

The mechanism by which muscle testing works is based upon both the intent of the person testing and the person being tested. Therefore, it is important that the language used be understandable and coherent. When people tell lies, the body responds with brain waves as well as changes in breathing, blood pressure, and heart rate, as measured by various biometric sensors (Abouelenien et al., 2014; Burzo et al., 2018).

Therefore, Adaptive Therapy will teach therapists how to use these scientific measures for differentiating between true and false answers, to guide the line of questioning and discussion during a therapy session. In much the same way, the body responds with a weaker muscle tone when a statement or question has a false or negative answer. On the other hand, when an individual tells the truth or gives an affirmative answer, the body produces a strong muscle response.

An Adaptive Therapist would be alerted to an emotional imbalance whenever a person tested weak when stating something positive. An example would be testing weak on the statement, "I want to live," and strong on the statement, "I want to die." For a person, believing this in their core would eventually lead to their death. Regardless of the imbalance found using Adaptive Therapy, there is a protocol employed in conjunction with applied kinesiology, in order to ensure that the process is truly being directed by the client and not by the practitioner.

How do people's muscles know what is true for them? After intensive research, Adaptive Therapists concluded that the answers to muscle testing were coming directly from the True Self that is repressed in the unconscious state. Finding this path to testing was a mind-expanding experience, as well as wonderfully empowering—it means that each person can align their conscious self with their True Self. Doing this type of alignment offers nothing less than success at every turn. And this is exactly what has happened for those who are well down this path.

The only way that the True Self, hidden in the unconscious, can express itself is by pushing an emotion to consciousness. It often pushes a positive feeling to consciousness; for example, an ocean breeze kissing your face probably produces warm, safe, or relaxed feelings depending upon your experience. If you almost drowned in a rip tide, chances are your feeling will not be positive, but instead you may experience anxiety, fear, or shortness of breath. Experiencing positive feelings will produce a connection with the breeze, and a desire for prolonging the good feeling as long as possible. With a negative experience, the immediate response would be to move away from the breeze, close the window, or leave the ocean-facing deck to conform to the underlying belief, "The ocean will kill you," also making it impossible to enjoy the ocean again.

Although this example would be uncommon for most people, there is a much more common experience: Rush hour traffic!

Do you feel trapped in rush hour traffic? Studies report that 90% of drivers feel anxious, irritated, frustrated, pressured, rushed, held back, or many other negative feelings, depending upon both the initial experience with rush hour traffic and subsequent reinforcing experiences with it.

Would you rather feel calm, content, or relaxed instead? You can by drilling down to find out what the core issue is that your True Self is bubbling up from the unconscious, alerting you that a core belief is being violated. In response to this stressor, stress hormones are being released in your body (Ursin & Eriksen, 2004; Reme et al., 2008).

To find out the core belief behind your response, you would ask yourself, "Why do I feel pressured when driving in rush hour traffic?" The answer could easily be: "I can't be late," or possibly "I'm never late." Why the feeling? Because you are about to break your rule "I'm never late" or "I can't be late" because the traffic is holding you up.

To correct the feeling and come back to being relaxed, you would change the belief into: "I no longer feel that I am never late" or "I feel that I am on time regardless of when I arrive."

To get to the core, a therapist would also examine why being on time is so important. Maybe underneath this is a need to be perfect, to be loved. But this example only addresses the behavioral level related to reactions to traffic. Each person's emotions and beliefs are linked to their experience; typically, no two interpretations of a similar experience are alike.

(Note: Adaptive Therapists do not use the emotion or the event in the reprogramming process. These are used to uncover the reason for the reactions and the perceptions, and then reprogram them.)

Therefore, Adaptive Therapy is testing the aspect of self that represents who we really are—our True Self. It directs the process of healing on the path that is most appropriate and at the pace that best serves the person. It is interesting that the device of muscle testing is a one-way communication system. Answers only come when asked. The True Self never asserts itself without permission. It is respectful of the unconscious agendas that are in place that block its expression. It will not violate a belief system as that would cause an imbalance. The True Self doesn't need to speak; it is already everything and yet, nothing. This can be difficult for humans to understand because we are governed by our physical aspects and external behaviors.

Adaptive Therapy would not have existed without applied kinesiology as the basic tool of investigation; however, now this tool can be replaced with biometric sensors and software. Most of the information revealed through applied kinesiology is impossible to receive in any other way. Even those who have come to Adaptive Therapy after practicing meditation for years have found this access process much more precise than anything they have ever experienced. Using muscle testing to access accurate meanings provides insight, opportunity for growth, and ability to change. These elements are not as easily obtainable in any other form. This is why Adaptive Therapy offers healing to everyone in a very deep and personal way.

Muscle testing/applied kinesiology is a method for accessing the inner knowing of a person, her/his True Self. It is used to test unconscious agendas that block the True Self. The intent of the people involved in the testing is paramount, because asking and then testing the True Self for what direction to take is quite different than making a statement; then muscle testing allows to see if the belief is held within the human aspect of self. Therefore, both therapist and client need to be clear in their communication, so they can verify where the answers are coming from.

Affirmations

Affirmations are used to change the programming held in the unconscious. An important aspect of affirmations that is often not recognized is the need to deprogram negative beliefs before putting in positive beliefs. Simply repeating a positive statement will conflict with the existing belief. Fortunately, most people are not able to establish the positive beliefs in the unconscious, thus protecting them from conflict due to cognitive dissonance. This section explores a method of extracting established perceptions and core issues, and replacing them with positive, desired ones.

Humans cannot mentally talk themselves out of acting on a core issue once it is triggered, no matter how they try. Automatic pilot is engaged and the ability to come up with fresh and creative responses has been shut down, because the person is in safety mode. This explains why people can look back at their behavior and wonder how they could have said or done what they did.

Adaptive Therapists formulate affirmations beginning with "I no longer feel…" and "I feel." The reason for using these phrases preceding a statement of the core belief or perception is to connect an emotion to the desired perceptions. As explained earlier, four elements are required to make change: trust in the person providing the change, emotion, repetition, and anticipating being accepted by one's tribe.

So, a set of affirmations would be: "I no longer feel that I am a victim" and "I feel that I am empowered."

Using affirmations like "I am intelligent" or "I am abundantly filled with everything I want" are superficial and do not make it past the barrier to the unconscious. They don't manifest much change. If they did, more average people would be excelling in the world, and be happy and fulfilled.

Also, in the deprogramming process it is important to tell the unconscious that you no longer believe what is in there; the word "No" is used to accomplish this. Some people have a resistance to this word being used with affirmations, saying that "No" is a negative word. The word "No" is not negative.

The last generation programmed children to believe it was negative because they didn't like to hear it said to them. In fact, it is a positive word that provides safety for those who use it appropriately. Even so, some say that the unconscious doesn't hear negative words. But this cannot be the case, as illustrated by all the "negative" programming that everyone has. To heal or perform at a higher level, negative programming needs to be replaced with positive, helpful beliefs. People also need to use some form of relaxation to lower the barrier between the conscious and the unconscious.

Mindfulness Breathing

Mindfulness breathing, when used with affirmations, influences the unconscious and assists it to perceive affirmations as a new, real experience. It also produces relaxation while the affirmations are "applied." The application of the affirmations is done by repeating them two to three times per day for two weeks. Other components of the technique reduce the defense mechanisms that resist reprogramming, give access to memories that are in opposition to the new beliefs, and allow the person to adopt the new beliefs by being conscious of the changes. As a result, perceptions and core beliefs formed earlier are updated just like a computer program.

The techniques used in Adaptive Therapy to change belief systems that limit life's experience when in homeostasis, or that cause stress when a belief system is violated, are relaxation and breathing while repeating the de-programming and re-programming statements (also known as "mantras"). These are part of the mindfulness technique. Below are the steps:

1. Find a quiet place.
2. Sit comfortably with hands resting on legs, palms up.
3. Take a deep breath in, feeling it rise from the soles of your feet, up your body, and out of the crown of your head; then on the exhale bring the air back into your body and release it through your throat.
4. The above is done while repeating the statements such as:
   "I no longer feel pressured to be better."
   "I feel at ease to be myself."
5. Repeat each statement twice, back-to-back.
6. Record your statements so that you won't be interrupted by looking at written text.
7. Repeat this process two times a day for two weeks.

References

Abouelenien, M, Pérez-Rosas, V, Mihalcea, R, Burzo, M. (2014) Deception detection using a multimodal approach. *ICMI '14: Proceedings of the 16th International Conference on Multimodal Interaction.* (pp. 58-65).

Burzo, M, Abouelenien, M, Pérez-Rosas, V, Mihalcea, R. Multimodal deception detection. (2018) *The Handbook of Multimodal-Multisensor Interfaces: Signal Processing, Architectures, and Detection of Emotion and Cognition, 2,* 419–453.

Reme, SE, Eriksen HR, Ursin H. (2008) Cognitive activation theory of stress—how are individual experiences mediated into biological systems? *SJWEH Supplements, 6*, 177-183.

Ursin H, Eriksen HR. (2004) The cognitive activation theory of stress. *Psychoneuroendocrinology, 29*(5), 567-592.

CHAPTER 4

Living Intentionally

Consciousness is simply a state of awareness—the more aware people are of what is going on within themselves, the more conscious they are. This means paying active attention to thoughts and feelings, to the inflection in someone's voice, and even to the energetic level of life. If people were conscious enough, they could literally talk to the wind, communicate with animals, and "hear" the thoughts of others. If people were able to become 100% conscious, they would experience being connected to all things at all levels, experiencing no difference between self, others, and the surrounding environment. The idea of separateness is simply a human concept, an illusion. It is not real on the energetic plane. Everything is one (Blanco et al., 2005; Saunders et al., 2010). The more people separate themselves from their surroundings, the more separate they are from the True Self, and the farther away they are from consciousness.

Asking the question "Why" leads to a more conscious state and connection to the True Self. "Why are things the way they are?" Seeking self-knowledge for any reason begins a journey, like a switch one has turned on that compels people to want to know more. Maslow's hierarchy of needs explains this as the drive to self-actualize. However, it's not only people who have food, clothing, and a home with a strong sense of self that wonder why or yearn for more meaning in life. In fact, usually pain, loss, or health problems compel a person to search for answers within. "Why do I feel this way?" "Why do I act this way?" Many people distract themselves from these problems by abusing drugs or alcohol, playing video games excessively, working 24/7, and other addictions.

Some say that they don't want to know who they are because they fear that others won't like or love them. They believe that they are protecting themselves by not knowing the truth, but in fact they already know the truth at an energetic level. Not acknowledging it consciously does not change the impact of the truth. Avoiding the truth, any truth, and thereby consciousness, will produce confusion. Energetically, all aspects of self are being bombarded with this knowing, while the conscious mind lives in denial. Everyone experiences this state of denial, but it is not a healthy one.

Here is an example: A person keeps getting fired from his jobs. Someone who wants to avoid knowing the truth will blame the boss, the requirements of the job, or say the boss didn't like him. Someone who wants to know the truth, and thereby circumvent a repetition of the pattern, will ask "Why?" With this truth, he could change his unconscious beliefs that block conscious connection with the True Self, so that a new course in the future could be laid down. The concept is simple, but many do not realize it. Individuals who want to avoid the truth would prefer to keep repeating the pattern and blame others for their problems, rather than taking responsibility for all that occurs in their lives.

Nothing happens *to* us, it happens *for* us; events allow us to grow, leading to our true nature, the actualization of our talents and a full life, thus contributing to our uniqueness.

The ultimate benefit of consciousness is that life will be richer, deeper, broader, and certainly calmer. This is because all events, feelings, thoughts, and so on, can be viewed as positive learning experiences and not bad ones. Because there is no blame associated with consciousness, there will be no fear of taking responsibility for what is co-created. Everything is fair at this level of awareness. Trust will also be highly developed. Even though we often cannot know in advance what truth we will learn in relation to an event or experience, we do know without a doubt that there is that truth. This kind of belief produces results, yet that doesn't even matter, because this kind of trust in the truth has no attachment to outcome. Belief trusts that whatever is delivered is exactly right, whether it be a gift of some kind or a loss of a friend.

Even people in Adaptive Therapy sometimes lose sight of the purpose of consciousness or enlightenment. Simply stated, the purpose " is not to get." It is not to get health or to have this or that. It is not to remove pain and suffering. It is not to get what one wants through the power of positive thinking. The purpose is knowing that what is received will be for the highest good of ALL: accepting what is serves us and others; acceptance is what will bring peace.

Desiring things or events is not wrong; it is the attachment to them that is detrimental. Have you ever wanted something so badly, received it, and then wished you never had gotten it? When living consciously, you will be able to confidently ask for what you want and then open your arms to receive it, convinced that what comes will serve everyone. Even if the result seems to be troublesome, like a difficult relationship, it has served all because there are many lessons to learn. It is of greater value to have challenges in our lives that propel us toward the lessons we need to learn within ourselves. Having "nice" friends who do not tell you the truth does not lead you to know yourself. Thank those who reveal to you clearly who you are, people who trigger changes within you that would serve you.

The benefits of being conscious are unlimited. Assertion of ego will not be necessary any longer. Confidence will reign, and therefore the facade of self-exaltation presented by ego will fall away. Genuineness will result. When living in this relaxed state, creativity will be greatly increased. And, most of all, living consciously means that people will truly know themselves.

The way to consciousness is to use all events, occurrences, feelings, thoughts, illness, and disease as a way to learn about

Self, and thereby increase the level of conscious awareness of Self. All life events, thoughts, and feelings are instructional, even positive ones. Look for the lesson and a sense of balance in response to every event in your life. When people find themselves overly jubilant, for example, it might be the response from within to a lack in their life. An example of this is being recognized for an achievement and then feeling more powerful as a result. The question to ask is what this experience is telling you. This example could indicate a possible lack of self-valuation, as the feeling of being more powerful was the result of receiving recognition. Being externally validated is fine, but the quality of the response to it, a dramatic sense of increased power, may indicate a need to examine what core issue is being triggered. Gratitude and humility would probably be the response of someone who had an adequate level of self-valuation.

Meditation is also another useful tool for increasing self-awareness. Some have thought that meditation is dangerous because the mind is being emptied, and therefore vulnerable to spirits. In fact, meditation is about setting aside judgment about thoughts or feelings that come up. Judgment is what is being removed, not our thoughts or feelings. Simply letting what comes up be, without effort to change or remove it, is what meditation teaches. This is necessary for seeking inner truth, listening to those thoughts and feelings without judgment, and figuring out what they are trying to tell you. Meditation is a way to listen to your inner voice, not to something outside of yourself. The practice of meditation is a beneficial support within Adaptive Therapy, for those who choose it.

In Adaptive Therapy, an increased level of consciousness is achieved through deprogramming and reprogramming of perceptions and core beliefs. This process leads to greater alignment of our consciousness with the True Self, so that we can live an intentional life. Living intentionally means to make choices in life rather than responding to what life brings. It is fun, actually, and creates resilience in crisis and empathy for the world's dilemmas. Living intentionally means engaging with every moment, all day long, by utilizing tools to maintain intentionality.

A path toward greater consciousness is open to all. Each person is responsible for his/her own progress. Once awakened, a truly conscious person will not judge others for where they are on their path, even if they appear to have not even begun walking it. No one knows someone else's heart, or his/her path. Truly, each person is on an individual journey, in communion with others.

Self-Help Method of Healing

Adaptive Therapy was developed through my own experience, through making the lifestyle changes, emotionally, physically, spiritually, and mentally, that brought about tremendous personal healing. Since its inception, Adaptive Therapy has been a self-help model of healing. This tradition continues; when taught, it becomes the tool that students and therapists use in their own process as they heal themselves. Adaptive Therapy is a self-help tool that clients can learn personally and apply to healing by accessing their inner wisdom. When people use Adaptive Therapy directly on themselves, they must learn how to self-test. This is accomplished by finger muscle testing or sometimes by pushing on their arms or legs. This muscle testing process is applied by asking "Yes" and "No" questions. Training for such a process is intensive because the development of integrity is crucial. Without personal integrity, it is impossible to get to the core of an issue. The person testing must want to know the truth, no matter what it is. There can be no fear or denial; otherwise, it will block the truth. This is why it is often necessary in early self-practice to get assistance from someone else who doesn't have the same issue. A component of the coming Therapist Assist device, called Third-I, will be helping clients to monitor and report results of their sessions in between sessions.

The Third-I is an app with a brain wave measurement tool that is being developed to replace the muscle testing process so that anyone can ask questions of the True Self; individuals can use responses to modify their perceptions and core beliefs.

Early research shows that with brainwave sensors, Adaptive Therapists are able to clearly and quickly differentiate between a "Yes" or "No" answer, and as a result can effectively direct the line of questioning to a person's core issue for modification. IAffirm, a 501(c)3 nonprofit, has been gearing up a team of scientists to design a study seeking evidence of successful questioning, including pre- and post-stress responses to a stressor to determine effectiveness of Adaptive Therapy. This study and others will be published in peer-reviewed journals and include the science underpinning Adaptive Therapy. Anecdotally, therapists know it works; people express dramatic change and attain improved health. The publication of research will make this knowledge widely available to the scientific community.

This area of research is focused on the stress response system (SRS) and measures a consciously known answer by a person to questions posed. This is used to validate or invalidate whether the answer is aligned with the person's unconscious, replicating the applied kinesiology process previously used during therapy sessions. In addition, stress levels are measured before and after the therapy session, and after a couple of weeks measured again to validate that the previously stressful situation is no longer triggering an elevated stress response. With the low cost and ready accessibility of such EEG measurement tools, this research can be conducted affordably and outside of a lab. This book describes the theories that underlie the research, which will touch on many different aspects of self-exploration.

References

Blanco, MA, Pendas, M, Francisco, E. (2005) Interacting quantum atoms: A correlated energy decomposition scheme based on the quantum theory of atoms in molecules. *J Chem Theory Comput, 1* (6), 1096–1109.

Saunders, S, Barrett, J, Kent, A, Wallace, D. (2010) *Many worlds?: Everett, quantum theory, and reality.* Oxford University Press. (pp 1-618)

CHAPTER 5

Addressing Health Conditions and Disease with Adaptive Therapy

Although Adaptive Therapy does not diagnose, treat, or prescribe medication, it does focus on any ache, pain, imbalance, stress, and even disease that people experience. It offers help and hope to people to improve their physical health by addressing emotional issues. Research has demonstrated that chronic stress has a significant effect on the immune system that ultimately may manifest as an illness (Cohen et al., 2012). The goal of Adaptive Therapy is to prevent disease by identifying areas of stress and helps individuals to adapt to stressors by modifying faulty perceptions and core issues.

The global COVID-19 pandemic added a new dimension to stress that has now become chronic; if not addressed, this stress will produce more illness and raise the cost of healthcare. Not only will it influence return to work (or not), it will cause core beliefs to be violated, thus triggering emotions that can lead to aches, pains, inability to concentrate, and ultimately, disease conditions. Prior to the pandemic, it was not in the consciousness of the average person that a virus could stop their life, alter their life, or take the life of loved ones so suddenly. As a result, people considered themselves relatively safe because most believed that they had a considerable amount of control over their lives. Overnight, that changed for everyone. So, what belief was suddenly adopted as a result of the pandemic? Even though people are different from each other in the process of encoding a belief based upon existing perceptions, life conditions, and core issues, virtually all adopted a new set of beliefs surrounding the personal impact of the pandemic.

Some people would have replaced, "I have control over how I live my life" with "I have no control over how I live my life; I'm at the mercy of germs." Perhaps they adopted beliefs such as "My whole life is up in the air" or "I have to stay home to be safe." Medical staff may have adopted the belief "I'm sacrificing my family for others," and those unwilling to adopt it may have left the healthcare field, or felt emotional pressure to leave.

How long do these beliefs last? Until something better comes along to replace them. Of course, these beliefs might become more moderate due to new learning, but for the most part, people are stuck with their new beliefs because the unconscious uses them for protection.

Those who have adopted the belief "I have to stay home to be safe" will have a negative feeling when they aren't able to get quickly back home. Those who view the virus and vaccine through misinformation such as "Don't trust science" will end up rejecting other government mandates in the future because of the programming that can occur through the media. By relying on what they view as a trusted source, their beliefs are shaped through the media's use of fear about losing their freedom, and by repetition. People need to guard their minds from this kind of media intrusion by asking "Why?" They need to reflect on these questions: "Why would the government try to take away my freedom?" "What is their motive?" "Why should I believe this source of information?"

The pandemic has created trauma for many people. Traumas have deep and long-lasting impact on individuals' ability to live without being triggered and re-triggered by similar events. People can be so traumatized that it shakes them to the core, which then could provoke an awakening event, compelling them to ask "Why?" Asking "Why?" helps people discover the True Self. It has led millions of people to ask themselves, "Is my life as I've known it something I want to continue, or should I do something else?" This process causes many people to move, change careers, stop working, and undergo multiple other personal changes.

Trauma actually offers an opportunity to re-invent the self, hopefully from the inside out based upon your True Self. This is the perfect time for getting help to discover who you are and adapt your life to the one you really want to live. This will ultimately reduce stress, make you healthier, and more at peace.

As mentioned earlier, something has changed radically in our world in the last few years. At base, this is the frequency and intensity of trauma. Most people during childhood and young adulthood experienced a few traumas that shaped the way they viewed the world, themselves, others, and their sense of how they are viewed by others. However, today people are faced with daily trauma. Even if you avoid the news, traumas like the pandemic have touched everyone's life. Mask-wearing and vaccine-taking are also traumatizing people.

Another source of trauma is related to the weather. You don't have to watch the news to know that weather has been changing and causing record damage, loss of life, and suffering. Road closures, closed federal lands, and smoke make evident the devastation that fires are causing during the now-extended fire season. Evacuations due to more powerful storms that drop record rain across a larger landscape also can't be ignored as major stressors in people's lives. And each of these, as they affect you and your loved ones, provide good opportunities to reinvent yourself.

What if you do watch the news? Well then, you are being traumatized every day as stories of war, gun violence, assassinations, coups toppling governments, inflation, political divisions, poverty, drought, loss of biodiversity, pollution, the latest on the COVID-19 pandemic, and so much more, mostly bad news, fills the public media. This news is delivered with elevated emotion, repeatedly, and with the goal for that media outlet to become your trusted source of information. Should you not watch the news? No, you certainly can, to stay up-to-date on what's going on; but guard your mind. The best way to guard is to ask, "Why is this happening?" "Is this really true?" And if so, "Why is it true?" Question everything and decide for yourself what you want to believe that aligns with who you really are, not who the media tells you that you should be.

This, of course, carries over to advertising. Probably everyone has noticed that advertising uses emotion, repeats itself with its own mantras, and uses words and imagery to build trust between viewers and their brand. These elements meet the criteria for programming both you and your kids! Music is used in commercials to elicit emotion, too. People who want to live consciously need ways to resist such media manipulation.

Here is an example from my life: One commercial I like because of the music is by a restaurant chain I would never go to because they don't serve what I consider healthy food. There is a cute dance scene with original music and it's very captivating, but it does not tempt me to go there. Why? Because I have programmed myself to only crave food that is healthy for me. To avoid temptation, I don't keep unhealthy foods in the house because my desire to run to the store has been nipped early on, so I don't go there to get it. Therefore, by modifying my core beliefs of what is good (healthy) for me and what is not, I can resist unhealthy food cravings or habits which could lead to serious health issues such as cardiovascular disease, diabetes, kidney disease, and many others.

Stress

Most people seek an Adaptive Therapist because they don't feel well, physically and/or emotionally. As a result of stress, they are no longer able to manage their condition. Up to 90% of doctor visits in the U.S. are stress-related as reported by The American Institute of Health and others (Salleh et al., 2008). Stress is a factor in five out of six leading causes of death, including heart disease, cancer, stroke, lower respiratory disease, and accidents (Stansfeld & Marmot, 2002; Soung & Kim, 2015; Booth et al., 2015; Pederson et al., 2010; Day et al., 2012).

This means that people are visiting doctors for the wrong reason and taking the doctor's time away from diagnosing and treating disease. Not only are most doctors not trained to address "stress" or "stressors," they have not considered stress to be a disease and hence find they are in the gap between mental and physical disease. Scientific literature validates that stress can lead to disease. By the time a person receives the diagnosis of disease, it's more difficult to reverse the disease than prevent it in the first place by reducing stress as the major contributing factor.

It is the hope, and intended work of this author, to change this situation. The goal is to increase help in addressing the stress-inducing pathway to disease by first naming chronic stress as a disease, simply by calling it a Stress Response Syndrome. A second step will be developing diagnostics to measure the allostatic load of those with this condition; allostatic load (AL) is the "wear and tear" on the body which accumulates as a person is exposed to repeated or chronic stress (Wikipedia). Conceptually, AL refers to the body's inability to adjust physiologically to stressors (Mair et al., 2011). AL mainly affects the cardiovascular, metabolic, and immune systems by disturbing the release of important biomarkers in the body (i.e., epinephrine, dehydroepiandrosterone sulphate, and cortisol) (Borrell & Crawford, 2011). It includes the physiological consequences of being exposed over time to fluctuating or heightened neural or neuroendocrine responses resulting from stress.

Ultimately, the goal of this author is to create a specialty in medical school education to train future doctors in scientific-backed alternative therapies that augment perception-modification. Healthcare, while armed with many new techniques and tools, has struggled with delivering therapies that are effective in addressing chronic stress. Adaptive Therapy is one solution, but not everyone wants to take the journey of introspection to change perceptions that lead to their disease, and many are too emotionally impaired to do so. Research at IAffirm will seek to identify emotional signatures using brainwave analysis to invent new "affect sublingual" medication to create a feeling or inhibit one, especially in emergency situations such as in suicide ideation, addiction, or other emotionally induced mental illness.

Consider the cigarette-smoking population. Why do they smoke? To reduce stress, many will say, at least until the craving starts again. However, it's a very unhealthy way to manage stress and smoking could lead to disease and lower life expectancy by at least 10 years (Jha et al., 2013). Many substances reduce stress temporarily, such as alcohol, psychedelics, prescription drugs, and others. Exercise, meditation, and yoga reduce stress, at least while people are performing those activities and for some time thereafter. Everyone has heard of "comfort food." Certainly, salty and sugary snacks reduce stress, though this can also produce disease. However, none of these coping methods can change the reason why a person has stress in the first place.

You can use relaxation techniques to explore the question, "Why do I feel stressed?" Make notes and then consult an Adaptive Therapist to permanently modify the perceptions and core beliefs that underlie your stress. Stress has been defined as any type of change that causes physical, emotional, or psychological strain. What is change? Here is an explanation many people can relate to.

Imagine being married to someone who was not raised like you, who does not share the same belief systems. This is a set-up for conflict and change is only possible by agreeing to adapt to each other's differences, namely by modifying perceptions and core beliefs. Some conflicting beliefs needing modification might be:

"I am a neatnik" vs. "I only organize myself on the weekend."

"I always pick up after myself" vs. "I don't have to pick up for myself because my mom/dad does it for me."

"I am a night person" vs. "I am a morning person."

"My parents were always there for me" vs. "My parents were always absent."

"I like a quiet house" vs. "I like a family full of commotion."

"I believe in myself" vs. "I don't believe in myself."

"I like alone time" vs. "I can't handle being alone."

As you can see, resolving these kinds of differences can be challenging and lead to many conflicts in a relationship if they aren't properly addressed.

Take the first set of conflicting beliefs above. Here is a couple living in a situation where one person is relaxed about how his/her things exist in their shared space, and the other is a neatnik who can't have anything out of place, in their view. Each will feel positive emotions when the environment conforms to his/her belief, and be relaxed about the situation. After the house has been cleaned on the weekend, things settle down. But by Tuesday or Wednesday, the neatnik is going to start feeling negative and expressing it in various ways, possibly starting with hints or joking, but ultimately by Friday expressing the negative emotion openly to their partner. For the purpose of this example, the neatnik would be experiencing the feeling of being disorganized.

The more relaxed partner is programmed to be neat on a weekly basis, not a constant basis, so he/she never violates the belief system of organizing things on the weekend; however, they will feel the impact from the other partner who wants more order. The relaxed partner will be the recipient of the hints, jokes, and the ultimate onslaught of blame, due to the neatnik's feelings of disorganization. This is a prime example of creating and experiencing stress. Both partners are now stressed.

If the relaxed partner was actually never taught to organize frequently, the situation would be far worse. So, what are the options for this couple?

1. The neatnik partner could pick up the slack Tuesday through to the weekend.

2. The more relaxed partner could be intimidated into doing more organization based upon the neatnik's requirements. But then his/her negative emotions would be triggered; instead of feeling relaxed, he/she may feel forced to do something which might result in negative behavior toward the partner who is perceived as forcing the clean-up actions.

3. The partners could design their own fix: perhaps the neatnik could choose to believe that their home is neat whether or not everything is always in its place, and the relaxed partner could change his/her belief, so it would not be necessary to wait until the weekend to get organized.

As you can see, this is an easy fix to resolve a small conflict that, if left unattended, will lead to resentment and potential loss of the relationship. And this is only ONE difference! Because of the differences in their belief systems, dissimilar people will struggle with conflict unless they navigate, adapt, and learn more about why their partner feels the way they do. Then they can opt to adopt their partner's perception and core belief. After all, some people have been reared to thrive better than others and each person can learn new ways of living, not through confrontation but through modification.

Not all stress is something to avoid. Some stress over a limited period of time will improve performance, such as running a race or taking an exam (Dhabhar, 2018). But prolonged stress will cause steroid hormones to do their damage and lead to serious health issues, or even death (Cohen et al., 2012).

The Relationship between a Specific Emotion, Core Belief and its Perceptions, and a Specific Disease Condition

Research in Adaptive Therapy has anecdotally found that, indeed, there are core beliefs that, when violated, will lead to a specific disease condition. Evidence-based research has also been conducted in this field (Mayne, 2001; Francis, 2006; Lee et al., 2017).

Research at IAffirm is underway to map emotions, perceptions, and core beliefs to genetic expressions to inform researchers, medical communities, and the general public of risk factors for disease, so that prevention can be implemented. It is highly valuable to establish the emotional risk factors for cancer, heart disease, high blood pressure, and many other conditions.

In Adaptive Therapy, cancer is related to a core belief, "I don't want to be here." This turns cancer into the killer that it is. An event, trauma, or situation leads to a core belief produced by a person's assessment of these experiences, resulting in a perception that basically says, "Do not ever do this again." However, if the person gets into that situation again and cannot get out, it will ultimately affect their gene expression, which could result in cellular changes, eventually leading to a diagnosis of cancer. Note that there are many different flavors of "I don't want to be here" because each person is unique, such as:

1. "I'm done, I'm out." (but you stay)
2. "I want a divorce." (but you don't get one)
3. "I quit." (but you don't)

Getting married could be an example of being in a situation that your personal rule formed long ago dictates "Don't do it." Getting married results in non-conformity to your core belief, if you grew up in a divorced family and it was so painful you swore off ever getting married. But there you go, you did it. Say you got divorced after this painful marriage, but then re-married a few years later. Now you're in the situation again, violating your core belief. The chronic stress responses that produce disease are continuing. It can be so difficult to grasp how our programming demands our adherence and how it punishes us if we get out of line. But we are human computers, after all—our programming leads inexorably to results.

While there are contributing factors like environmental toxins and hereditary tendencies, alterations in gene expression can lead to the occurrence of disease. Adaptive Therapy considers emotions to be the basis of disease, generated by the violation of core programming. When someone has made a decision based upon an event, and then does not follow through, this violates a core belief and will produce the negative feeling, the trigger. Since depression is a common precursor to cancer, as research shows (Spiegel & Giese-Davis, 2003), Adaptive Therapists believe that depression is the emotion that is "expressed" both emotionally and genetically. This affects the body's ability to function, lowering protective mechanisms and allowing the cellular changes to take place that lead to cancer.

Not everyone dies from cancer, and it has been found that people who remain positive are more likely to survive (Creagan, 1997). Adaptive Therapy hypothesizes that survival is not due to a positive attitude, but that survival is more likely among the type of people who decide that cancer is their teacher, who want to know why and reinvent themselves. Such people stop violating their perceptions and reduce their stressors by making changes in their mind or their situation. An example could be a spouse that the client wants to divorce but recommits to upon learning (adapting) how caring their spouse really is; the client goes through surgery, chemotherapy, radiation, and/or other cancer cell-targeting therapies, and on to recovery, with the spouse right there giving support.

Receiving a diagnosis of cancer is a trauma to everyone, including those around the client. Outcomes would improve dramatically if clients and their families would participate in Adaptive Therapy as part of their treatment plan.

Migraines occur when someone has the belief "I don't want to, or I can't confront differences," including having too much to deal with, feeling overwhelmed, or needing to just time out. When faced with opposing situations, the feeling of being "shut out" or "ignored" bubbles up while producing the symptoms of migraine including visual effects and ultimately the headache itself. Why? To stop the person from confronting the differences in front of him/her. A migraine typically sends someone to bed or, at a minimum, to a quiet, dark room to wait for it to end.

Diabetes is a disease that affects 371 million people worldwide, and at least another 187 million do not even know they have the disease, according to the International Diabetes

Federation (IDF). What do diabetics have in common? According to Adaptive Therapy research, it is a core belief of self-hate. Why? There are many reasons for self-hate, including comparing oneself with others, and viewing the self as "fat," "too dark," "ugly," "stupid," "too short," and a myriad of other reasons why a person feels negative. Hating oneself produces hateful behavior to self and probably to others in certain circumstances.

However, as long as the perception of why someone hates themselves is not violated, stressful emotions are not triggered.

So, what would violate the self-hate core belief? Having friends (and being jealous of them), having loving kids, an appreciative partner, a good job, an accepting church or group, or anything that might trigger "You're not so bad after all." Who teaches someone to hate themselves? Some parents may contribute, but the most likely source is the pecking order in middle school. Only a few girls and guys considered the most socially desirable or attractive get away with being privileged; the rest are less-than and sometimes hate-able, not deserving to be loved. Advertising to youth feeds into these attitudes by producing the behavior of comparison, resulting in "I'm not good enough." Reinforced experiences that are similar could ultimately drive youth to decide that they hate themselves. As long as they isolate themselves and reject love, attention, attraction, or commitment, people can probably avoid triggering the feeling of being cared about and worth loving. As can readily be seen, people in this paradox are damned if they do and damned if they don't. Adaptive Therapy would help a client to reframe the core belief of self-hate and the perceptions that reinforce it.

High blood pressure, from the Adaptive Therapy perspective, is the result of people being simultaneously conflicted over being a positive person and a negative person, with regards to how they view their life, the world, themselves, and others. The number of adults aged 30–79 years with hypertension has increased from 650 million to 1.28 billion in the last 30 years, according to the first comprehensive global analysis of trends in hypertension prevalence, detection, treatment, and control. The study was led by the Imperial College London and The World Health Organization (WHO), and recently published in *The Lancet* (World Health Organization, 2021).

While it is easy to say this increase in hypertension is the result of the sped-up world and stress associated with rapid change, Adaptive Therapy postulates that it's a direct result of declining social and financial equity. Due to repeated fluctuations in political and economic conditions, people who formerly were positive and hopeful realized that the world had changed, and the security they once felt might be gone forever. Attitudes of loss, frustration, and mistrust fly against a positive attitude, thus many people are caught in between.

It is tough to face what appears to be reality, which seems completely justified, and then take action to change it. This is exactly why people don't like to change. To reach a strong opinion takes time and giving up your opinions feels like lying to yourself.

Here is an example of a gentle, kind, and loving way to reframe conflicting beliefs. Adaptive Therapy doesn't take sides and seeks only to help people adapt to what is, not what they wish was.

Belief: Science is my guide for making decisions.

Opposing belief: I don't trust science to guide my decisions.

These can both be changed with affirmations:

"I no longer feel that science is my guide for making decisions" can be changed to "I feel that my inner Self guides my decisions."

"I no longer feel that I don't trust science to guide my decisions" can be changed to "I feel that my inner Self guides my decisions."

In this example, people are adapting to a mutually agreeable solution, to listen to sources outside the self and then listen to the True Self to make decisions. No one person has to be right or wrong, which then silences the conflict, and harmony can once again ensue.

Science is not perfect and should not be completely trusted, just as social media shouldn't either. Science and chemical companies have many lawsuits to prove this point. Social media acknowledge false claims. So the ideal way to make a decision is by gathering information, asking why, and then listening to your True Self. The bottom line is that people have to stop blaming each other for their own feelings, and must take responsibility for their choices instead.

Change, especially when it is happening suddenly, causes the violation of core beliefs. Everyone must adapt to change in order to avoid stress, illness, and losing the ability to thrive. How will anyone survive if the working class suddenly is replaced by robots? What if a nuclear accident actually happens on a global scale? How do you get your head around quantum travel when it arrives, as advanced technology folds space to reduce distance between locations? Again, people must adapt to be resilient, to live well, and to be able to help others find their way.

From the Adaptive Therapy perspective, people with multiple sclerosis (MS) have a core belief that they don't want to be helped. They enjoy their independence fiercely and don't want to give it up. When violated, this person probably feels inadequate, inducing changes in genetic expression to produce the disease. As the disease becomes more debilitating, greater help will be needed. Remission is common in this disease and ultimately could be related to the level of independence the client is able to attain. Once realizing there are emotional components to disease conditions, clients can reinvent themselves and change their core beliefs for renewal.

Probably the most popular request for how to "fix a problem" is around weight loss. What is the core belief behind obesity? "I'm too busy." This means that a person who can't seem to lose weight can't be in the present; can't take time to care for self; can't relax; and is uptight. Even if a person does manage to relax, this will result in negative feelings like "anxiety" or "impatience to get going again" or "agitated." So, an overweight person is an agitated person trying to relax who is probably binge-eating to suppress feeling agitated, or a person rushing around to get things done, including multi-tasking to a fault. Sound familiar? This problem needs attention now because overweight and obese conditions are expected in 85% of the US population by 2030 (Harvard TH Chan School of Public Health, 2019).

References

Booth J, Connelly L, Lawrence M, Chalmers C, Joice S, Becker C, Dougall N. (2015). Evidence of perceived psychosocial stress as a risk factor for stroke in adults: a meta-analysis. *BMC Neurology, 15* (233), 1-12.

Borrell, LN, Crawford, ND. (2011). Social disparities in periodontisis among US adults: The effects of Allostatic Load. *Journal of Epidemiology and Community Health, 65*(2), 144-149.

Cohen, S, Janicki-Deverts, D, Doyle, WJ, Miller, GE, Frank, E, Rabin, BS, Turner, RB. (2012). Chronic stress, glucocorticoid receptor resistance, inflammation, and disease risk. *PNAS 109* (16), 5995-5999.

Creagan, ET. (1997). Attitude and disposition: Do they make a difference in cancer survival? *Mayo Clinic Proceedings, 72*(2), 160-164.

Day A, Brasher K, Bridger RS. (2012). Accident proneness revisited: The role of psychological stress and cognitive failure. *Accidents Analysis & Prevention, 49*, 532-535.

Dhabhar, FS. (2018). The short-term stress response— Mother nature's mechanism for enhancing protection and performance under conditions of threat, challenge, and opportunity. Front *Neuroendocrinol*, 49, 175-192.

Francis, LE. (2006). Emotions and health. *Handbook of the Sociology of Emotions Springer*. (pp 591-610).

Harvard TH Chan School of Public Health (2019). https://www.hsph.harvard.edu/news/press-releases/half-of-us-to-have-obesity-by-2030.

International Diabetes Federation. https://www.idf.org/news/240:diabetes-now-affects-one-in-10-adults-world wide.html)

Jha, P, Ramasundarahettige, C, Landsman, V, Rostron, B, Thun, M, Anderson, RN, McAfee, T, Peto, R. (2013). 21st-century hazards of smoking and benefits of cessation in the United States. *N Engl J Med*, 368, 341-350.

Lee, Y-S, Jung, W-M, Jang, H, Kim, S, Chung, S-Y, Chae, Y. (2017). The dynamic relationship between emotional and physical states: an observational study of personal health records. *Neuropsychiatr Dis Treat*, 13, 411–419.

Mayne, TJ. (2001). Emotions and health. In T. J. Mayne & G. A. Bonanno (Eds.), *Emotions: Current issues and future directions*. Guilford Press. (pp. 361–397).

Mair, CA, Cutchin, MP, Kristen Peek, M. (2011). Allostatic load in an environmental riskscape: The role of stressors and gender. *Health & Place*, 978-987.

Pedersen A, Zachariae R, Bovbjerg D. (2010). Influence of psychological stress on upper respiratory infection—a meta-analysis of prospective studies. *Psychosomatic Med*, 72 (8), 823-832.

Salleh MR. (2008). Life event, stress and illness. *Malays J Med Sci, 15*(4), 9-18.

Soung NM, Kim, BY. (2015). Psychological stress and cancer. *J Anal Sci Technol, 6* (30), 1-6.

Spiegel, D, Giese-Davis, J. (2003). Depression and cancer: mechanisms and disease progression. *Biol Psych, 54*(3), 269-282.

Stansfeld, S A, Marmot, MG (Eds.). (2002). *Stress and the heart: Psychosocial pathways to coronary heart disease.* BMJ Books.

The American Institute of Health. https://www.stress.org/americas-1-health-problem.

Wikipedia. https://en.wikipedia.org/wiki/Allostatic_load

World Health Organization (2021). https://www.who.int/news/item/25-08-2021-more-than-700-million-people-with-untreated-hypertension. WHO/Imperial College London press release from The Lancet, Worldwide trends in hypertension prevalence and progress in treatment and control from 1990 to 2019: a pooled analysis of 1201 population-representative studies with 104 million participants. *The Lancet*, 398, 957-980.

CHAPTER 6

Finding a Purpose

Adaptive Therapy's final goal, once people are directing their lives from the True Self, is to aid them in finding their purpose. "What can I do with what I know and who I am? Where can I contribute best?" Most people on the planet are too busy working, maintaining a home, putting food on the table, and responding to stress to even consider how they can help anyone else. This probably explains why people give donations to help others—because they want to help but giving money is the only way they know how. But what most people need is more than just money. They need activists involved in changing the things that are not working in the world. If you yearn to help others, then find a way to become part of the solution by adapting to your life's reality and making new choices.

An example of making new choices is simply realizing that having more does not make you happy. Getting more things does bring certain satisfaction temporarily but not over the long term. Having "more" has its price, probably increasing the need to work more hours. And once you have something you have to maintain it. A house is an acquisition that you have to keep paying for. Consider the lifestyle you are living and make some new choices, changing your core beliefs to live a life you embrace as being in alignment with who you are.

People have been under the impression that working hard, saving money, and following the rules will eventually reduce the pressure they are facing, and will give them the freedom to make their own choices. This is what companies want you to believe so that you will work hard, be dedicated, provide businesses with "bank loans" through money from your savings account, and convince you that you need what they produce. If this loop stops, and people get off the treadmill created by business and perpetuated by leaders and investors, the economy will collapse. The U.S. is built on this model. Continuing the loop, however, makes the rich richer, the poor poorer, and the middle class stuck on the treadmill. Even during the pandemic, Wall Street increased its value because of the stimulus money that the government pumped into the economy to keep it from collapsing. It was basically done to keep people buying the stuff companies produce. This book isn't about how an economy should work but is about deciding for yourself, choosing how you want to work. Do you really want to sacrifice your life or quality of life for an employer that is only interested in selling more products?

It's important for people to ask themselves, "Why am I working? Does it fulfill me?" If not, they should take a look at what would be fulfilling and adapt their behavior to pursue it. They must be sure to change their core beliefs and perceptions, however. If someone wants to be an artist but his/her perception is "All artists are starving," that person probably won't do well pursuing an artistic career without changing core beliefs.

Learn where your talent lies. What comes easily to you? What are your interests? Combine these two things and seek counseling on what career would suit you best. The world is wide open to opportunities, if you just look, investigate, and trust.

Removing Blocks to Purpose

Everyone has blocks to overcome. As you journey toward your purpose, you will encounter them. You won't know initially what the block is because it's hidden in your unconscious programming. However, you can use the feeling that bubbles up to identify the blocks, root them out, and replace them with empowering perceptions and core beliefs.

An example of a block might be related to losing weight. You are on a diet using an app that's working. You don't snack at night anymore and you've cut down on alcoholic beverages to almost none. But you can't make yourself exercise. You plan it but then you get distracted, and time gets away from you. This is how you know you have a block. In this case, it's the feeling of resistance that causes procrastination. You know you're doing it, but you can't stop it.

The first question to ask is, "Why am I feeling resistance and procrastinating when I know I want to exercise?"

Maybe it is helpful to look at what you are choosing to do instead of exercise. Maybe you choose to work, for example. This means you derive something more from working than exercising. Perhaps it's because work provides you more pleasure. You can see why you would then choose work. This perception needs to be modified and then you drill down to the core issue, which in this example could easily be that "Life is boring." Again, everyone is unique with core beliefs that are all their own, developed through life's experiences.

Although losing weight is not in itself a purpose, it just might be a goal to achieve your purpose. If you want to be a leader, then you need to be an example of what your followers want to be like. Losing weight in our society has been overrated, but living with a healthy weight is the goal, not to be skinny. If skinny is your goal, look for perceptions and the core issues that shape harmful behavior such as anorexia or bulimia.

A True Self-Designed Life

Adaptive Therapy offers a way to modify behavior, reduce emotional stress, and improve health and well-being. This means that everyone has the opportunity to re-invent themselves to become what they want, instead of only being what they are programmed to be. Why just "be" when you can "Be" an expression of your True Self? Acknowledging what you feel can lead to a life-changing discovery about self that, once modified, can eliminate frequent negative feelings and change unwanted behavior. This can ultimately produce a True Self-designed life with purpose.

This book gives impetus for further research and hopefully will inspire multi-disciplinary inquiry to connect the dots between our emotional states and our biological systems. This will advance the acceptance of evidence-based preventive healthcare initiatives. Modern healthcare has an opportunity to reduce cost, increase access, and greatly improve outcomes. Stress reduction programs need to be the first line of defense against disease. Prevention of disease will preserve the talents and free the contributions of medical professionals to more efficiently diagnose and treat disease.

Finally, Adaptive Therapy is compatible with modern healthcare and follows many other cognitive-behavioral approaches that strive to explain human emotions, behaviors, and beliefs, and their links to illness. This book postulates what Adaptive Therapists believe to be an end-to-end solution for those suffering emotionally, physically, and behaviorally.

Adaptive Therapists welcome input, collaboration, and effort from others to expand healthcare access to all people, with the goal of providing global access.

Visit: https://IAffirm.org to learn more.

CHAPTER 7

Future Growth of Adaptive Therapy

Integration with Technology in a Brain-Computer Interface (BCI)

The integration of multiple elements of technology with therapeutic approaches has been increasing steadily. Adaptive Therapy currently is using brain-wave measurements to validate the accuracy and scope of assessments, and to monitor effectiveness of therapies for changing belief and perception patterns. Self-Directed Living, the outcome of Adaptive Therapy, depends on adapting to the changing world; there are significant consequences if people cannot adapt. Adaptive Therapy is the modern world's answer to a high-velocity life because it helps people slow down, become more aware, amplify intuition, and change perceptions that are not aligned with their environment.

Help with adaptation comes in many forms and will benefit the world in many ways. That's the beauty of technology: the ability to replicate and extend possibilities. Some of those ways are therapeutic, such as creating a more informed lifestyle, elevating awareness, and inhibiting the stress response system that is often chronically "on" and often leads to disease. Other solutions for high-stress lifestyles can build upon this, including personal identity security. Help can come from a new medical specialty called Adaptive Medicine, focused on treating chronic stress with no side effects, including the development of affect catalyst medicines created from emotional signatures, and a universal, non-verbal language.

Medicines of the Future

The medical field has been stuck in a rut for a long time, and this rut has cost many lives and too much money to justify how it operates. It avoids looking at causation and focuses on case management, primarily treatment. New medications are created but humans weren't designed to be chemically altered, which often leads to some form of rejection by the body, known as side effects. The medical field must also adapt to survive and hopefully develop a new approach to medicine. The model I'm proposing will reduce the cost of healthcare, improve outcomes, and pave the way for more research into non-invasive and side effect-free treatments and medications.

Modern medicine must look at the whole of a person, not just a part. Doing so paves the way to deliver healthcare using a new paradigm, knowing that the mind influences physiology and physiology influences the mind. I propose that this new approach needs its own medical specialty, Adaptive Medicine, which can help humans adapt in a dynamic, unpredictable world.

The American Psychology Association (2020) reported:

> Our 2020 survey is different. It reveals that Americans have been profoundly affected by the COVID-19 pandemic, and that the external factors Americans have listed in previous years as significant sources of stress remain present and problematic. These compounding stressors are having real consequences on our minds and bodies. It is the unusual combination of these factors and the persistent drumbeat of a crisis that shows no sign of abating that is leading APA to sound the alarm: **We are facing a national mental health crisis that could yield serious health and social consequences for years to come.**

This is happening because people simply don't know how to adapt when things change too often and too quickly. They become unnerved, because humans operate based upon the predictability contained within the reservoir of learned experience that allows them to operate fairly autonomously. It was impossible to prepare people emotionally for COVID-19. The pandemic super-charged a global reset for many who had the time to reflect on what is important. The pandemic was a catalyst for people, partners, and families to make new choices for reducing stress, improving connection, and finding purpose.

Others became overwhelmed by the added layer of stress from the pandemic and collapsed, resulting in a "war-like" response of defensiveness, as if overrun by an enemy. No longer able to cope, they lost access to their inner knowing and lashed out when challenged. They became easily influenced by those who "feel their pain," mistakenly accepting such statements as genuine without question. This is a frightening response as it can lead to the surrender of one's identity.

And what values were driving them? To claw back what they had, and fight for it, feeling completely justified because they had been wronged by the government, people in power, and by anyone who disagrees with them.

The Stress Problem

Research reveals that up to 80% of doctor visits in the U.S. are stress-related, wasting precious healthcare resources on appointments and tests that lead to no solid diagnosis, with doctors shrugging their shoulders saying, "It's probably just stress." There are not enough mental health therapists to help those needing help with stress, because they have their hands full dealing with mental disorders and addiction.

US Percentage of Population by 2030

Obesity	85%
Diabetes	14%
Mental Health Disorder	50%
Cardiovascular Disease	45%
Chronic Disease Condition	49%

And yet...

- Alarming emotions turn on your body's internal stress response system.

- Environment-shifting causes millions of biochemical signals to tell your entire body to be on red alert.

- Prolonged stress activation pushes your body's organs into dysregulation.

- If the stress response cycle is not stopped, this dysregulation will foster chronic disease and mental instability.

Stress is Killing Us: Humans are becoming overly stressed. Rather than being mentally capable of choosing and building a life worth living, they can only respond to their stress, day in and day out, which is making them sick.

The Potential of Adaptive Medicine

Humans are like computers but with the emotions and the ability to make creative decisions. Operations continue without difficulty if the environment remains threat-free, as was common before the technology age. Humans are no longer living in a threat-free environment due to global, regional, local and personal conflict, calamities, social division, lack of resources, and loss of trust.

New techniques, tools, and medicines are needed to monitor and interrupt auto-activation of the Stress Response System (SRS). These tools can differentiate between a real threat and a pseudo threat. They are used to assess the environment for potential SRS activation and give warning if risk is detected. Yet other treatments will include affect catalyst medicines (from emotion-signatures) to deactivate the SRS, without side effects. The goal is to help humanity to humanely adapt more quickly to an ever-changing world, reduce disease conditions, and lower the cost of healthcare.

Lost in the Gap: Stress-caused human suffering is growing with no widely effective treatment plan in sight. There are temporary solutions but no actual resolution on the horizon. Unhealthy examples include substance abuse, excessive gaming, entertainment, overeating, or even harm to self or others. Many work in excess to avoid facing the stress of life, or mistakenly assume that making more money will solve their stress. Others reach out for help from books, apps, and practitioners using meditation, yoga, and other mindfulness techniques. While these are helpful, relief is still only temporary, until another mass shooting, relationship conflict, or COVID-19 outbreak impacts life.

A Medical System Solution: Establishing Adaptive Medicine as a medical specialty that focuses on the diagnosis and treatment of chronic SRS activation will address the gap between stress and disease conditions, both mental and physiological. This is an urgently needed paradigm shift for humanity. This will reduce the burden and cost of healthcare and improve outcomes. The medical industry has a specialty called Preventive Medicine but does not address stress specifically, although this is what is needed. Instead, their concept of "prevention" is to get regular exams to "catch it early," and not to actually prevent disease.

The Adaptive Medicine curriculum can be developed for medical schools to implement a diagnostic and treatment protocol for this newly named "disease," such as SRS Syndrome. This curriculum will prepare future doctors with the skill sets to diagnose, treat, and track results of stress prevention, leveraging evidence-based tools, techniques, and medicines that produce a healthier population. Once the curriculum is ready, the American Medical Association (AMA) can include the treatment of stress as a condition requiring education and specialty licensure.

Addressing Home Insecurity

While most of the focus of Adaptive Therapy is devoted to improving physical and psychological health, with the right business model, the homelessness issue can also be tackled through Adaptive Therapy. This approach is one where dignity is restored, training is implemented, and personal growth is at the core of renewal. I propose to consider home security using the lens of Adaptive Therapy.

First, homelessness is not a housing problem. I think many people would agree with that, but do they know what it is then? I propose that it's a failure to survive within society for one reason or another; hence, a group has developed the program called Revive to acknowledge the problem and create a gateway back to society for those without homes. This problem is global, and it seems as though governments lack not only the resources to deal with it, but also the will.

Revive will re-home people in sustainable housing in a communal style with each member having a role to perform in service to the community. Each earns a small salary for service and for Sunday tours of the sustainable community from sold tickets. The community also generates revenue from builders that replicate the model across the world. No government money is required, which means no strings either. The community creates and enforces its own rules. Members are encouraged to stay 12-18 months to rehabilitate and reform unproductive behaviors. Each learns how to live in society, which includes learning how to manage money, how to raise kids, how to cook, how to get and retain a job, and how to contribute to the common good of humanity. Most importantly, each person will plan and create a path to sustainable living with a healthy mind upon exiting the program. Each will have a trust account where 50% of their earnings are saved for them, so upon exit each will have a start-over fund.

Personal Security

For far too long, humans have been viewed by opportunist groups and businesses as a commodity, with mind-manipulation all around them without their permission. The technology being developed by Adaptive Therapy to facilitate awareness and alignment with the environment also offers a brain-computer interface that warns of the threat of undue influence.

A personal security product provides a warning system to amplify the innate human "internal voice" that has been desensitized by the constant barrage of life's events. Through this augmentation, the personal security product enhances intuition so that important decisions can be made, over time or on demand instantly. IAffirm's proprietary algorithms circumvent the process of believing something without question, through the amplification of conscious awareness of the "internal voice," allowing free will to make the choice instead.

Society has turned up the volume on mind-manipulation, so humans also need to amplify their responses. If they don't amplify their responses, they might drown in a sea of too much information, surrendering their identity to anyone who wants to exploit them.

The Metaverse

While most people don't think of the Metaverse as something they will have to deal with, in 5 to 10 years everyone will be facing this technology for virtual and augmented reality. What safeguards are there to prevent exploitation? This is not at the top of most people's minds because it's the opposite of the goals presented in this environment. It's an environment of influence on steroids, manipulating people to consume goods and services or to shape beliefs and opinions.

Hence, we are designing a product for people to offer protection in the Metaverse, with the ability to cloak presence, speak a universal language so everyone knows where danger is, and to provide personal security checks so there is no manipulation. This technology will not be welcomed by groups and businesses that want to manipulate, but there is enough of a cry from people demanding ethics to provide entry for such protective products. Details of these products are included in the patents filed.

There are hundreds of products that will be built with the algorithms created to access unconscious awareness, measuring brain waves and interpreting them to inform users of their environment, externally, internally, and virtually.

For More Information and Help

This book has probably piqued your interest to examine your own beliefs and perceptions that limit your life. If so, you can do so in several ways. First, contact us at IAffirm.org to find a therapist to work with directly. Second, you can reach out to a certified life coach who can work with you, using the Third-I app and headset (which measures your brainwaves to provide accurate assessment). And third, you can use the Third-I app and headset on your own, engaging with the chatbot to assess, identify blocking beliefs, and reprogram your unconscious mind.

Visit https://genoemote.com to follow our progress.

References

American Psychological Association. (2020). https://www.apa .org/news/press/releases/stress/2020/report-october.

CASE STUDY 1

Trust and Rejection

Adult female adopted at birth unable to fully trust anyone, experiencing rejection by most people having power over her, like her boss or anyone in a relationship with her.

A 50-year-old woman presented still suffering from the loss of her family of origin, never having known them. The little she learned about them is painful; she was given away because the family already had four children and she was conceived as the result of an affair. In this example, she is called Jane.

Since therapists know how the early years shape people's lives, the first question asked of Jane was, "How was your family that adopted you?" She relayed how they had treated her well, and she always felt like they were her parents. But there was this lingering feeling, this hole that felt empty in her. The session began by addressing the perceptions that were created as a result of being adopted, seeking to identify the core issues underlying them. Another objective was to explore if she was aware of experiences while she was in utero.

Jane did recall emotions while in utero, including her mother's experiences of grief, loss, and shame. These emotions related to three different core issues before birth. As a result, she sought out situations that explained why she believed them, as she grew up into a young woman. Jane also reinforced these core beliefs with perceptions developed from similar events.

Core Issues:

- I am empty. (grief)
- I don't have a choice. (loss)
- I am a bad person. (shame)

Perceptions:

(I am empty/grief)

- No one really wants me.
- I don't have much to offer.
- I don't know who I am.
- I'm missing something.

(I don't have a choice/loss)

- I am stuck in my life.
- I can't do what I want to do.

(I am a bad person/shame)

- I made an unforgivable mistake.
- I don't deserve to have anything.

The core issues were set in utero. So, imagine Jane growing up in her adoptive family and having an alcoholic dad who shushed the kids if ever they interrupted his television programs, while he was drinking. She was regularly punished for making noise and being herself, so the feeling of loss, attached to the core belief "I don't have a choice," tagged the perception from these "shush" events to "I can't do what I want." Other events occurred during a marriage that demanded she work 24/7 to avoid financial ruin; this led to Jane developing another perception related to the feeling of loss, and to the core issue "I don't have a choice."

These perceptions direct people's lives and behavior, and if they make new choices that don't conform to the established and reinforced perception, stress occurs to push them back to conforming. Such perceptions can ruin people's lives, make them miserable, and derail anything they might try to do differently.

Therapists should note that some perceptions can be projected onto others. For example, since Jane perceived that her birth mother made an unforgiveable mistake, Jane may define certain acts toward her by someone else close to her as being unforgivable.

This case study is intended to introduce therapists to the elements to address in a therapy session. It does not explain the process of arriving at these core issues or perceptions. The next case study will include this process.

CASE STUDY 2

Feeling Ignored and Betrayed

Core issue of being ignored, with feelings of betrayal when people take "digs" at the person.

This case study is based on the author's own self-work. To be an effective therapist, one must do their own deep dive to modify programming that limits the ability to help others. Therapists cannot help clients with problems they themselves have not resolved.

I've done self-work using thousands of programs for almost 40 years. One in particular came up recently related to perceiving that people "dig" at me; they take little digs (comments, behaviors) to hurt me purposely. At least, that's how it felt. Because I reacted to it, I explored why.

To begin the unraveling process into the core issue, I started with the question, "How do I feel when people take a dig at me?"

Answer: Betrayed

Here is an overview of the process displayed in this case study.

Perception Development & Reinforcement

1. WHEN SOMEONE DOES A "DIG" AT ME (SITUATION)

2. APPRAISAL SYSTEM SEARCHES FOR PREVIOUS EVENT(S) THAT CONTAIN AT LEAST 2 COMMON CHARACTERISTICS – IN THIS EXAMPLE THEY ARE: CONFIDENT IN WHAT I HAVE TO OFFER + BEING SLIGHTED

ORIGINAL EVENT

BETRAYED

CHILDHOOD EXPERIENCE OF RECOGNIZING **MY TALENT**, SAYING "LOOK AT ME!" AND **PARENTS IGNORING** ME SO I DON'T GET A BIG HEAD.

I THINK TOO MUCH OF MYSELF.

BETRAYED

MY SISTER LIKES TO REMIND ME HOW "DIFFERENT" I AM AND IT'S **NOT A COMPLIMENT**; ALSO SUGGESTED RECENTLY I'M NOT AGING WELL YET I'M PROUD OF HOW I LOOK AND FEEL FOR MY AGE.

PEOPLE TEAR ME DOWN.

BETRAYED

REINFORCED

WHEN MY BOARD SAID WE NEEDED A STAR-POWER CEO, NOT ME, I **WROTE AN EXIT OPERATIONS MANUAL** WHICH WAS **NOT EVEN OPENED** BY ANYONE AT THE HAND-OFF MEETING, OR AFTERWARDS.

I'M NOT A STAR.

BETRAYED

RECENTLY A BUSINESS PARTNER HIRED A CONSULTANT TO FIGURE OUT HOW TO GO TO MARKET, **BY-PASSING MY 40 YEARS OF ENTREPRENEURIAL EXPERIENCE.**

I HAVE NOTHING TO CONTRIBUTE.

BETRAYED

WHILE IN EUROPE TEACHING MY HUSBAND SIGNALED IT WAS MY TURN TO **PRESENT** AND HE STATED, " NOW IT'S TIME FOR ALEX TO **MAKE A FOOL OF HERSELF!**"

I'M THE BUT OF A JOKE.

3. TRIGGERS BETRAYED FEELING GENERATING BEHAVIORAL OPTIONS: ◄

4.
1. KEEP MY HEAD DOWN; AVOID GREATNESSS; ACCOMPLISHMENT.
2. STAND UP FOR MYSELF AND HATE ON OTHERS FOR WHAT THEY "DO" (BETRAYED) TO ME.

THIS EVIDENCE PROVES MY CORE IDENTITY: "NO ONE RECOGNIZES MY GENIUS."

The second question then was, "Why do I feel betrayed when someone takes a 'dig' at me?"

The best answer to this question for me was "I don't have anything to contribute." This was the result of experiences during grade school, such as being called on by the teacher who asked, "So, Alex, what do you think?" I shuddered and shook my head in terror, hoping he would move on to someone else. He did, but not before saying, "Oh, so you don't think?" As a result, I came to believe "I don't have anything to contribute," a new perception that became attached to and reinforced a core belief formed in early childhood.

Perceptions of an event are formed by assessing, cognitively and unconsciously, the result of the event. In this case, it was very painful, and hence the perception created was to make me avoid repeating it, if at all possible.

Core issue (core belief): People ignore me because my parents would ignore me whenever I said, "Hey, look at me, look at what I can do!" Their motivation for ignoring me was to keep me from getting a "big head," which explains why I have to either be quiet and cover myself up, keep my head down, OR stand up and ask for recognition if the audience is ignoring me. All that I wanted from my parents was validation that I could do whatever I put my mind to. I had the ability in me innately and I had to overcome the programming to experience this in my life without stress or betrayal. This experience caused me to doubt myself and, as a result, my core identity and my perception of myself was altered.

The next question was "Why do you think that you have nothing to contribute?"

Answer: "I'm the butt of a joke."

This new perception was developed as I stood up at an event to talk about books for sale to the audience. My husband at the time said, "Now Alex can come up and make a fool of herself." He thought it was funny… I felt completely betrayed by him, and this event tagged a new perception to my existing core issue of being ignored, and feeling betrayed.

The next question was "Why do you think that you are the butt of a joke?"

Answer: "I'm not a star."

The reason for this is because I'd run a company as a CEO and was replaced by the Board because I was not a "star-powered CEO." I wrote an operating manual so that the new CEO could take over the company, which took me many days to prepare. I made copies and distributed them, but they were recycled quickly and as a result, I relived once again my core issue.

The next question was "Why do I think I'm not a star?"

Answer: "I think too much of myself."

For example, my sister actively took me down a peg or two by looking at an old photo of me saying, "Time hasn't been very kind to you, has it?" And she objected to my clothing style as being something she wouldn't be caught dead in. But that's my sissy. So, these experiences circled around again to the core issue.

The next question was "Why do I believe that I think too much about myself?"

Answer: "Because people ignore me." This brings the process to the core issue, being ignored.

Adaptive Therapy Techniques

The goals of Adaptive Therapy are to modify or re-program limiting beliefs, perceptions, and feelings. Using affirmations to make these changes is one basic tool. Taking the perceptions from my personal example, these could be modified with the following affirmations.

Perception: "I don't have anything to contribute."
Affirmations to modify this include:

- I no longer think that I have nothing to contribute.
- I think that I have a great deal to contribute.

Perception: "I'm the butt of a joke."
Affirmations to modify this:

- I no longer think that I'm the butt of a joke.
- I think I am admired.

Perception: "I'm not a star."
Affirmations to modify this:

- I no longer think that I'm not a star.
- I think that I'm a genius.

Perception: "I think too much of myself."
Affirmations to modify this:

- I no longer believe that I think too much of myself.
- I believe that I view myself realistically.

Core Issue/Belief: People ignore me.
Affirmations to modify this:

- I no longer believe that people ignore me.
- I believe that people pay attention to me.

As you can see in each reinforcing event, the common thread is *being ignored* in many of its forms. Here is how each perception was related to this core belief (issue/identity):

> Nothing to contribute: I wished the teacher would have ignored me; I perceived that I had nothing to contribute.
> Butt of the joke: I was excited to speak at the event, but what I had to say was quickly shot down so my value could again be ignored.
> Not a star: I was completely ignored and felt betrayed.
> Think too much of myself: My sister had taken me down with digs, which would get me to conform to my core belief of being ignored. She was ignoring my positive aspects, and focusing instead on the negative.

All I ever wanted was to be seen for my talents and abilities. Now I am.

CASE STUDY 3
Stress and Confidence Issues

Female doctor in her late 30s presenting with stress surrounding confidence in her ability at work, helping clients.

This recent client was fascinating because her limiting core belief involved some DNA memory from generations of women "programmed" to be useless. Using a series of "why" questions led to the discovery that her childhood was marked by neglect, because her mother was absent and expected her to take care of her younger sister, who was two years old, while she was just five years old. The children were left home alone all day. As a young child, the client had no words to explain or understand that what was happening was wrong or inappropriate, although she remembered that she felt afraid.

Prior to experiencing this series of events in her medical practice where she worried that she might mis-diagnose or mis-treat someone, she inherited the core belief that she was useless. This understanding came about through dialogue and using applied kinesiology to access her unconscious mind to validate the line of questioning. This was passed down from her mother and from her mother's mother, both repeating the same outcome—failing to succeed in any endeavor in their lives. The client's mom was actually going to school to try to advance her situation in life. In fact, she demanded that the family move to California so she could go to school, thinking that would be the ticket out of her useless life. But it did not work, and she never found a fulfilling career, thus continuing her struggle to thrive. Her daughter, my client, also found herself in a similar situation, saying that no matter how much she studied and learned, it was never enough to provide a path to thriving, or any sense of success. She continued struggling to make ends meet in her private medical practice.

Below are the affirmations that have turned her life around to the point of restarting her practice in a new place, one that is more aligned with who she is and where she could find a home that is the right fit as well. She is now on her path to thriving.

- I no longer feel that I don't know enough to safely perform my work.
- I feel I know enough to safely perform my work.
- I no longer feel that I can't take care of myself.
- I feel very capable of taking care of myself.
- I no longer feel that I am useless.
- I feel that I am useful.
- I no longer feel that I act upon the genetically inherited trait from my mother regarding usefulness.
- I feel free from acting upon the genetically inherited trait from my mother regarding usefulness.

CASE STUDY 4

Male presenting with Non-Hodgkin's Lymphoma

25+ year old male presenting with non-Hodgkin's lymphoma.

This young man came to me by referral from a client that I'd helped with a health problem. This case dates back more than 20 years. I thought it would be valuable to present an example of a failure, to examine the reasons why Adaptive Therapy may not be effective.

Little did I know at the time that I also had the core issue related to cancer, as did this client. I didn't learn this until seven years ago, when a cancerous tumor was found in my left lung by chance. I worked with this client for several months, until one day I got a call from his wife that he had passed away. I was devastated and began to question my work, mostly because I helped most people, most of the time.

Later, when I had my own cancer scare, I came to understand that therapists cannot effectively work with a client on a core issue that is not clear in them. I realized I could not help this client in the past because of my own perceptions that led to a similar outcome, cancer. This has motivated me to continue my own personal work as often as possible.

It is useful to dig into the topic of cancer since it's so devastating to so many families. In some form or another, a person who develops cancer has a core issue involving "I don't want to be here."

In my case, I'd been going through a very tough situation at work. At the same time, I was sitting at my desk looking out the window, watching a light snow coming down, saying to myself, "I'm so excited to be here for Christmas, with such a beautiful view, and running my own great company." I was feeling fully at home, finally.

This brought me to a full stop, of course. This was violating a core belief of mine that I developed in childhood under the roof of a fanatically religious mother, "I can't wait to leave here." I hated my childhood from age 12 to 18; six years of trauma was followed by drugging and drinking to reduce the stress of lying and pretending to be a good girl while doing the opposite as much as possible. My mother didn't intend to damage my psyche, because she was doing what her church told her to do to save my soul: "Break her will."

After leaving home at 18, glad to "get out," I repeated six-year stints in a number of six-year relationships that I also left without realizing that I was always motivated to "get out," but not really knowing why. I would always look at these relationships and find fault, instead of examining them in order to understand why they failed. Finally, in my late 20s I read my first book about healing because I was feeling sick, smoking three packs of cigarettes a day and drinking 10 cups of coffee to sustain my anorexic behavior. I decided I had to choose between life and death, so I chose life. I started my journey toward the Self by reading *The Road Less Traveled* (Peck, 2012). This was my turning point. Then I was introduced to the world of applied kinesiology in my early 30s, the foundation of Adaptive Therapy that I used to heal myself while developing the process.

I'm no longer waiting to find a way out, like I did in childhood. I'm no longer waiting to reach an end point. I am now committed to the long term, wherever I am. I notice too that I love where I live and don't plan to move again, even if I eventually may relocate. I'm helping my son, who is differently abled, and I intend to continue that for the rest of my life. And I am committed to Adaptive Therapy and helping others learn, teach, and share it, without a time limit. Instead of anticipating retiring, I'm retired already but have a wonderful project to work on—the growth of Adaptive Therapy!

So, if you find a client that you can't help, sit with yourself. Discover how you might be blocking yourself from helping them. I've found during a session that I can tell if I am clear. If I'm not, I'll put off working on the issue with the client until the next time I see them, so that I can address the blockage. Only then can I help them fully. Even though I could struggle through with a client when I have a blockage, it's not really fair to them, so I respect their right for me to be fully present during their sessions instead.

When my cancer was discovered, I'd been working 6-12 months on "getting back to my company," where I'd been ousted, which I believe triggered the cancer. In my experience, wanting to go back is dangerous. It's been quite the life of leaving and going back for me, including with the husband I dated off and on over 25 years, left, got back together with, and separated from again. While I can blame my ex-spouse by saying "It's due to his bipolar disease," that's not fair or true; our issue really stemmed from my perpetual need to "get out." I have this need to go back in order to be able to leave again. Talk about crazy, right?

I believe it's essential to understand how people's perceptions are different. What others see as crazy behavior, that is obviously harmful to everyone around them, does not seem crazy within the affected person's perceptions. That person is being driven to re-enact the past, with no control over it, to preserve and reinforce their core beliefs. People are always looking for more situations that reinforce the core issue to make it stronger, and to protect it more deeply (this is what the unconscious programming assumes, although it is not true).

Here is a breakdown of the emotions and the perceptions attached to the core belief, "I have to get out."

> Question to discover the specific emotion related to the core issue: "How did I feel being at the mercy of a religious fanatic whose goal was to break my spirit?"
> The feeling: Helpless.

First question to drill down into the perceptions: "Why do I feel helpless when at the mercy of a religious fanatic bent on breaking my spirit?"

Answer: "I can't wait to leave."

Affirmations to reverse or reprogram these perceptions and emotions:

"I no longer feel that I can't wait to leave."

"I feel content to stay."

Next question: "Why do you feel that you can't wait to leave?"

Answer: "I have no choice."

Affirmations to reverse or reprogram these perceptions and emotions:

"I no longer feel I have no choice."

"I feel I do have free choice."

Next question: "Why do I believe I had no choice?"

Answer: "People will never change."

Affirmations to reverse or reprogram these perceptions and emotions:

"I no longer feel that people will never change."

"I feel that people want to change."

Next question: "Why do I think that people will never change?"

Answer: "We all have an ego to protect."

Affirmations to reverse or reprogram these perceptions and emotions:

"I no longer feel that we all have an ego to protect."

"I feel that we have a Real Self to engage."

Next question: "Why do I believe we have an ego to protect?"

Answer: "My spirit will be broken."
Affirmations to reverse or reprogram these perceptions and emotions:

> "I no longer feel that my spirit will be broken."
>
> "I feel that my spirit is alive and well."

Next question: "Why do you feel that you spirit will be broken?"
Answer: "I'm under attack."
Affirmations to reverse or reprogram these perceptions and emotions:

> "I no longer feel that I'm under attack."
>
> "I feel at peace with everyone, and everyone is at peace with me."

Next question: "Why do you feel under attack?"
Answer: "I am a mistake."
Affirmations to reverse or reprogram these perceptions and emotions:

> "I no longer feel that I am a problem."
>
> "I feel that I am a solution."

Note that the perceptions are behavioral in nature, and when you reach the core issue (identity), it will be a decisive statement about self, others, or others' beliefs about self.

My mother and I resolved many issues while she was alive. She even studied Adaptive Therapy and did sessions with me, which was wonderful. No, it was never perfect, but we could enjoy each other's company and learn from each other, which is what's important. However, she did stay committed to her church until the end.

Reference

Peck, MS. (2012). The Road Less Traveled: A New Psychology of Love, Traditional Values, and Spiritual Growth. Touchstone. https://www.amazon.com/Road-Less-Traveled -Timeless-Traditional.

CASE STUDY 5

The "Perfect" Family

The perfect family. Addict came to address why he was an addict since he came from the perfect family; how could he be so screwed up?

While I agree that addiction is a chemical imbalance in the brain, and that it is a disease, I still believe that there is a great deal of work that can be done to ease the guilt, shame, and consequences of addictive behavior. This client will be called Joel.

Joel grew up in a family that felt normal, with rules and guidance every step of the way. In fact, Joel received very positive programming that would lead to a life well-lived, just like the lives his parents had created. All was well until Joel reached 12 years of age.

Joel began to hang out with friends who did not get the beneficial upbringing he had. While Joel didn't want to follow suit with what his friends were doing, he wanted to continue being accepted by his friends and so went along. He first started smoking cigarettes in between classes. Then, feeling guilty about doing something he knew was wrong, he started drinking, a little at first and then more to numb his feelings about what he was doing. Not only did he know what he was doing was wrong, but he was also fighting feelings of guilt and shame as well. This led to dependence on substances to feel OK about life as he was choosing to live it, a life that was violating the programming instilled by his parents.

I suspect, after seeing many kids going through the "anxiety" of separation from their parents, that they use substances or do things to try and ignore their upbringing. Emotions are very potent influencers of behavior, for good or not so good. As a result, something needs to be done to either change back to childhood programming or suppress emotions with drugs, alcohol, sex, video games, shopping, or any combination thereof.

The human brain has all the chemicals it needs to power feelings that have immense impact on the body. Just recall the last time you were suddenly shocked by a near accident, when your heart felt like it was in your throat, right? Well, that's an emotional reaction that triggers a physiological response. Many other emotions also invoke behaviors; often the only way out of experiencing these emotions is to avoid them by numbing the body and mind.

Joel ultimately returned to his programming of living wholesomely by reprogramming perceptions that didn't match his goals. Now he lives on track to becoming who he wants to be, and he has mended his relationship with his parents.

It is my hope that this work can lead to helping those in recovery to address the programming that they have covered up. This could help them find peace by living compatibly with their core beliefs, without triggering the emotional responses that might push them back into conformity with addictive behaviors.

CASE STUDY 6

Self-Doubt

Adult male with lingering self-doubt developed during grade school; diagnosed with attention deficit disorder (ADD) and medicated; special learning classes

This client was 15 years old at his first appointment with me. At this time, he was on medication and in a special school program designed to help him learn. He was doing fairly well in his new learning environment. Later he returned as a client at age 40 to address lingering issues of feeling "different" related to how he experienced the trauma of learning differently.

For the purpose of this case study, the client will be called Jeremy. His case is probably the most comprehensive I've had with a client, and it's an important example to realize how many perceptions can be tied to a core belief and tagged with a specific emotion. Each perception occurred through a reinforcing event, and due to Jeremy's learning difficulties during years of school, this demonstrates how damaging these experiences can be. Fortunately, Jeremy is considered "high functioning" today and takes great joy in learning.

Jeremy did not realize at first that he was different in the way he learned. In second grade, teachers and administrators approached him and his parents to suggest that he may have a learning disability. This was a surprise to Jeremy.

He was tested and this confirmed that he had ADD, and Ritalin was prescribed. To provide some context and understand how Jeremy's identity was formed as a result, it's important to know his parents' backgrounds. Mom came from a family where advanced education was highly valued; in fact, if you couldn't attain it, you were deemed abnormal. Dad was a successful business leader who was highly educated. When mom and dad were told of their son's learning challenges, their hearts sank along with their hopes for him.

Jeremy understood through his parents' reaction that "Life was going to be extra hard for him." This set him up to feel that his "life was set in stone," with a certain outcome determined because he had this ADD diagnosis.

His core issue was that people didn't pay attention to him, because their focus was on how to "fix" him from their own perspectives, instead of asking young Jeremy "How can we help you?" Without casting blame on the parents, it would have been almost impossible for them to hide feelings of disappointment around their own situation, having a learning-disabled child in a family like theirs. "How are we ever going to tell my parents?" the mom might say. Dad would also harbor feelings that his son would not ever be able to achieve a high level of business acumen. And since this was their first child, their expectations would have been great!

The process of Jeremy's healing involved dealing with difficult perceptions derived from repeated learning events, such as boarding a bus for school that was designated for "disabled students" and struggling to learn in a group. The therapy process when Jeremy was age 40 helped him to remove self-limiting beliefs and behaviors follows.

The conversation started about something completely different than Jeremy's learning disabilities. Jeremy brought up an issue he was having while reading different books on the subject of meditation. He was confused about which one to believe because they did not all agree, and even books by the same authors would contradict themselves.

The Adaptive Therapy process started here with the question, "How does it make you feel when you have multiple authorities on one topic that contradict themselves and each other?"

Jeremy answered: "Frustrated."

The next question then was, "Why do you feel frustrated when sources contradict themselves and each other?"

A number of possibilities were narrowed down to: "I don't know what to believe when my sources don't agree with themselves or others."

Affirmations (deprogramming and reprogramming statements) were applied to root out the limiting belief and to replace it with what Jeremy wanted to believe, as follows:

"I no longer feel that I don't know what to believe when my sources don't agree."

"I feel that I know what to believe independently of my sources."

The next question is always about the belief that was just changed: "Why do you feel (or felt like) you could not believe your sources when they don't agree?"

After some testing, the process revealed that Jeremy didn't consider a philosophy valuable if it was not consistent. But this perception is limiting because philosophies can change as new things are learned. So Jeremy modified his beliefs with these affirmations:

"I no longer feel that if a philosophy isn't consistent there is no value in it."

"I feel that inconsistencies in philosophies offer opportunities for new understanding."

Next question, "Why do you feel that if a philosophy isn't consistent there is no value in it?"

Jeremy had lived many years believing that his life was set in stone, so he projected this onto others; in this case, he believed that philosophies also should be set in stone and not inconsistent. He modified his beliefs with these affirmations:

"I no longer feel that my foundation in life is set in stone."

"I feel that my foundation in life is built upon the field of possibility."

I'm sure you can see the value in this monumental change for Jeremy, how freeing it was.

Next question, "Why do you believe that your foundation in life is set in stone?"

Jeremy learned that he could be successful in learning one-on-one and by following the mantra, "Settle down, pay attention, and try harder." This was a new perception developed that reinforced the need to be fixed in place to succeed. It also helped him avoid the feeling of frustration that was attached to this perception and core issue. He modified his beliefs with these affirmations:

> "I no longer feel that I need to settle down, pay attention and try harder."
>
> "I feel appreciated when I behave according to my nature."

Next question, "Why do you believe that you should settle down, pay attention, and try harder?"

Answer: "Because there is only one way to learn."

Jeremy modified his beliefs with these affirmations:

> "I no longer feel that there is only one way to learn."
>
> "I feel that there are many ways to learn."

Next question, "Why do you feel that there is only one way to learn?"

Answer: "I feel that order comes from compliant behavior."

He modified his beliefs with these affirmations:

> "I no longer feel that order comes from compliant behavior."
>
> "I feel that order comes from the understanding of each other's ideas."

Next question, "Why do you believe that order comes from compliant behavior?"

Answer: "Because people don't know how to control themselves."

He modified his beliefs with these affirmations:

> "I no longer feel that people don't know how to control themselves."

> "I feel that people know how to empower each other."

Next question, "Why do you feel that people don't know how to control themselves?"

Answer: "People blame others for their problems."

He modified his beliefs with these affirmations:

> "I no longer feel that people blame others for their problems."

> "I feel that people take responsibility for their problems."

The next question was the one whose answer led to the core issue to which these perceptions were connected: "Why do you believe that people blame others for their problems?"

Answer: "Because people don't pay attention."

Again, Jeremy used deprogramming and reprogramming affirmations to modify his core belief about "not paying attention":

> "I no longer feel that people don't pay attention."

> "I feel that people pay attention."

This session revealed that Jeremy's frustration about inconsistencies in philosophies were the result of "people not paying attention," because if someone was paying attention, they wouldn't contradict themselves or peers in the same field without explaining why there are conflicting ideas. After resolution, Jeremy became more settled about different views based upon the same facts.

When drilling down to the core issue, you won't know where you are going during the process, but after you arrive it makes total sense. That's how you know you have gotten to the core issue. Remember core issues (identity) are how people view the self, others, and the world, or how they perceive that others view them.

ACKNOWLEDGEMENT

I want to thank every client and student, thousands of them, individually, as well as every person in my life who has taught me how to be my best self; I would like to especially acknowledge three people who have influenced me to commit to writing this book. First, and because she is my own flesh, my daughter who I birthed at 41 years of age asked me to leave behind a legacy of my life's work. She missed out on me because of this work, for which I've had to make amends. This book and my work are forever branded with her footprint, to go on into infinity reminding her of me in perpetuity; gifting her with the words "my mommy created that."

Then there are two clients who I've known for about 35 years, a mother and a son, Pam Hawes and Tom Hunden. We lost touch after my 18-year career as a therapist when I decided to live a self-designed life that I had created, drawing from my personal work. This involves visual technology, developing software that includes video preview patents (a

YouTube norm now). We reconnected about two years ago and Pam inspired me with these words: "Don't let this work die with you."

That seed from Pam took hold in combination with Tom's commitment to this work. Combined with Vedic meditation, it has changed his life and shaped him into the leader he now is within the field of self-reformation. The purpose of this work is to change psycho-social systems and methods that are ingrained in dead-end repetition, to new ways of thinking, exploration, and evolution, leading ultimately to personal evolvement and the capacity to carry one's life's work forward.

There are no words for how I feel about each of you, the many; the gratefulness I have is profound. But I will ask you to celebrate it all by starting your own journey to the True Self.

It's fascinating and rewarding. Go for it, for you.

ABOUT AUTHOR

Alexandrea Day has blended two careers as an Adaptive Therapist and visual technologist over 18 years each, to create a range of products that serve humanity. These include integrating self-awareness apps and EEG technology to support self-directed leadership, living, and therapy.

Alexandrea, an author, educator, and patent-holder, has spent a lifetime working with thousands of clients, teaching hundreds the Adaptive Therapy process through her Washington State Vocational School. She traveled globally to teach the techniques of Adaptive Therapy to individuals, healthcare professionals, and licensed therapists.

While Alexandrea's education is embedded in psychology, she left university in her third year to pursue the development of her own unique process of identifying and modifying limiting beliefs in the unconscious, creating the process now known as Adaptive Therapy. Her theories that humans are programmed computers that are re-programmable is supported by scientific literature and demonstrated in this book. This process of re-programming frees people from their limiting beliefs and paves the way to change behaviors, to excel in performance, and to attain health and well-being—permanently.

During Alexandrea's 18 years as a visual technologist, she produced thousands of corporate and event videos, filming with her national team and editing in-house with professional editors. She built software for a DIY video ad creation product; the latter even spurred a call from Google to visit their Silicon Valley campus Patents were granted to her that demonstrate her forward thinking, with a focus on improving the user experience. The preview video you see across YouTube now was envisioned by Alexandrea 10 years ago. In essence, Alexandrea's career has been a combination of 1) helping others, 2) keeping things simple and understandable, and 3) forward thinking beyond and without limits. This has given her the ability to ideate and create innovative products that benefit others. Her final work brings it all to market as her legacy.

Alexandrea is also founder of IAffirm, a 501 (c) 3 non-profit, formed to carry out her legacy project, ensuring that Adaptive Therapy will be sustained into the future so it continues to improve the human condition. IAffirm addresses the gap between medical and mental disease treatments, measures the impact of psychosocial events that cause stress, and provides evidence-based and effective treatment plans. This is accomplished through conducting research, and authoring educational products for GenoEmote, the for-profit sister company that exclusively builds products for humanity.

Meta-Brain: Reprogramming the Unconscious for Self-Directed Living is the Adaptive Theory solution for the modern world. Our non-stop lives are killing us, and there is currently no treatment. This situation is what Alexandrea has set out to change, including a pocket therapist for personal use; curriculum for medical schools to establish a specialty called Adaptive Medicine; and developing emotion-based pharmaceuticals, in partnership with like-minded mission leaders.